Refuge and Strength

PRAYERS FOR THE MILITARY AND THEIR FAMILIES

Written and Compiled by
Theodore W. Edwards, Jr.
CDR, CHC, USN (Ret.)

CHURCH PUBLISHING
an imprint of
Church Publishing Incorporated, New York

Church Publishing Incorporated
445 Fifth Avenue
New York, NY 10016
www.churchpublishing.org

5 4 3 2 1

Contents

Foreword

Heavenly Father, in you we live and move and have our being: We humbly pray you so to guide and govern us by your Holy Spirit, that in all the cares and occupations of our life we may not forget you, but may remember that we are ever walking in your sight; through Jesus Christ our Lord. Amen. —Book of Common Prayer (1979)

There is one way to pray and worship in the safety of homeland and homeport: in the company of family and friends and in a stately building with beautiful music. But the profession of arms takes one away from the comforts of home and habit and into a constrained environment where the need for religious support is high and resources are thin. This volume attempts to deliver religious resources to Americans in the uniformed services of the United States and to their families in the context of deployment. Deploying is what we do—we all do.

The intent is to assemble resources into a compact volume suitable for portable and expeditionary use when far from home on our country's business—at sea and overseas.

This book, together with the Bible, equips Christian pilgrims in uniform to be well prepared for the exercise of their constitutional right of religious expression wherever duty may dictate. Each chapter begins with a short discussion of the concerns that are addressed with the resources provided in the chapter.

Many of the prayers are of unknown and anonymous origin, but we thank those unacclaimed authors for their beautiful ways of communicating God's presence and assurance.

God's blessings go with all who read and use this book—abroad and at home.

A final thought, from the Scriptures: "I hereby command you: Be strong and courageous; do not be frightened or dismayed, for the Lord your God is with you wherever you go" (Joshua 1:9).

Chaplain Ted Edwards
CDR, CHC, USN (Ret.)
The Feast of St. Cornelius the Centurion
4 February 2008

Parrish, Florida

A Few Things to Know about Religion While Deploying

BEFORE DEPLOYING

Either your command has a unit chaplain or there is a chaplain responsible for providing opportunities for religious expression within your unit. There are also some individuals who have been appointed to serve as the lay leader for a particular religious expression. Get to know these people and find ways to support their work even if they are very different in religious practice from your own. The point is that you are not without religious resources and opportunities while deployed. The second point is that you can provide a great service to your command and the people within it by serving as that appointed lay leader and gathering resources to support worship, religious education, and Christian fellowship before you head out.

Your chaplain cannot provide for your needs if those needs are not known; nevertheless, your chaplain is responsible to provide opportunities for religious expression for all who request it. The chaplain will directly provide religious expression as authorized by the chaplain's endorsing faith community and facilitate opportunity for those that cannot be provided directly. If your chaplain's practice is so very different from your own, gather together several others with needs similar to your own and become the appointed leader. Once appointed, get training and equipment as needed before you deploy. It is very hard to do so after deploying. Take this book with you. Use it.

WHILE DEPLOYED

Support your chaplain's religious program the best you can, no matter what that chaplain's faith group endorsement. Chaplains respond to support with enthusiasm for what you do that supports servicemembers beyond the chaplain's direct religious authority.

Seek out other members of your faith community and others who share a common interest with you. Besides sharing religious common ground, they may form a fine core group for touring the great religious and cultural sites of the world when you are free to enjoy and visit these places.

Visiting foreign countries or ports is a wonderful opportunity to gather a group together and make a church expedition on Sunday. Especially for faith communities with worldwide activity, these will be the best opportunities of a lifetime to learn and experience more about your faith community. It is a profound experience to worship with your faith community in a foreign language and to receive their hospitality. Your faith group may publish a directory to help you find local foreign contacts.

Send letters and photographs to your home congregation. It is a blessed experience to pray for them and to be prayed for by them.

Remember this essential thing: the greatest stresses for both deployers and families are the first and last months of deployment. The adjustments to family systems and relationships are significant, especially for first-time deployers. Do not take them lightly or assume that family separation is a natural process that takes care of itself.

RETURN AND REUNION
WHEN THE DEPLOYMENT ENDS

The world did not stop turning while you were away for weeks or even a year. There will be a great many unexpected surprises in the first days home—some pleasant and some upsetting. Do not expect to adjust all at once, and do not expect the return adjustment to be easy on your family either.

For those with spouses or other committed relationships, remember this concept: "We are falling in love all over again." It is completely false to assume that anybody can pick up where they left off after a lengthy time away. Begin slowly and take time to court each other.

Let your spouse who stayed home with all the family activity tell all the stories in the first days home. Your stories matter and are interesting, but they will keep. Let the home stories be told first. Those stories will help you readjust to being home. When they ask for your stories, it is time to start telling them.

Let the children climb all over you before you focus on your spouse. The children will be back at play soon enough, and you can start falling in love again.

Your family systems all adjusted to your absence, and most of them now work quite well without you. Do not be insulted by their successful adjustment. It is good to let these systems keep working, because you will probably deploy again before long.

Visit and reconnect with your friends soon. Some may have transferred while you were away or be preparing to transfer soon. Friends are a valuable possession, and friendships need cultivation. They want to see you as much as you want to see them.

Be careful driving your car until your rusty driving skills are recovered. A very common mistake is to assume that your skills are as good as they were before you left and then to suffer an accident in the first days back from deployment. If your car was in storage, get it serviced right away. Check to make sure your license, registration, and insurance did not expire while you were gone.

Remember to bring home presents. They are expected. Make them very special. Remember that the real present is you yourself—safe and home again.

During the Day

Today is here, and it is the only day we can do anything about right now. Today will have its own joys and frustrations. There will probably be surprises, both pleasant and unpleasant. What better way to begin this day than with joy and praise from the 100th Psalm. That should set the tone for the rest of this day!

Psalm 100

Be joyful in the Lord, all you lands; *
    serve the Lord with gladness
    and come before his presence with a song.

Know this: The Lord himself is God; *
    he himself has made us, and we are his;
    we are his people and the sheep of his pasture.

Enter his gates with thanksgiving;
go into his courts with praise; *
   give thanks to him and call upon his Name.

For the Lord is good;
   his mercy is everlasting; *
   and his faithfulness endures from age to age.

*Since today will have its own joys and frustrations,
let's do the best with what we have at hand.*

This is another day, O Lord.
I know not what it will bring forth, but make me
   ready, Lord, for whatever it may be.
If I am to stand up, help me to stand bravely.
If I am to sit still, help me to sit quietly.
If I am to lie low, help me to do it patiently.
And if I am to do nothing, let me do it gallantly.
Make these words more than words, and give me
   the Spirit of Jesus. Amen.

One of the great things about being far from home, if there is anything good about it, is the opportunity to focus on what is right before us and not invest a lot of worry in what is beyond our reach anyway. Jesus counseled his disciples not to become victims of worry. That good counsel is available to us, so stop to read and maybe memorize Matthew 6:25–34:

"Therefore I tell you, do not worry about your life, what you will eat or what you will drink, or about your body, what you will wear. Is not life more than food, and the body more than clothing? Look at the birds of the air; they neither sow nor reap nor gather into barns, and yet your heavenly Father feeds them. Are you not of more value than they? And can any of you by worrying add a single hour to your span of life? And why do you worry about clothing? Consider the lilies of the field, how they grow; they neither toil nor spin, yet I tell you, even Solomon in all his glory was not clothed like one of these. But if God so clothes the grass of the field, which is alive today and tomorrow is thrown into the oven, will he not much more clothe you—you of little faith? Therefore do not worry, saying, 'What will we eat?' or 'What will we drink?' or 'What will we wear?' For it is the Gentiles who strive for all these things; and indeed your heavenly Father

knows that you need all these things. But strive first
for the kingdom of God and his righteousness, and
all these things will be given to you as well. So do
not worry about tomorrow, for tomorrow will bring
worries of its own. Today's trouble is enough for
today."

Lord, thou knowest how busy we must be this day;
if we forget thee, do not forget us, for Jesus Christ's
sake. Amen.

*Let's be thankful to God for the beginning of this
day, because, God knows, any of us might not have
made it to this day. Not only is our work dangerous,
but we have all taken silly risks and made foolhardy
mistakes in the past that could have killed us. None-
theless, God has seen fit to bring us to this day and
has always been faithful to us in the past—so we
begin with thanksgivings for this day:*

Lord God, almighty and everlasting Father, you have brought us in safety to this new day: Preserve us with your mighty power, that we may not fall into sin, nor be overcome by adversity; and in all we do, direct us to the fulfilling of your purpose; through Jesus Christ our Lord. Amen.

O Lord, support us all the day long of this
    troublous life,
until the shadows lengthen, and the evening comes,
and the busy world is hushed,
and the fever of life is over,
and our work is done.
Then in thy mercy, grant us a safe lodging,
    and a holy rest,
and peace at the last. Amen.

Show us, God our Father, some way of serving you this day by helping someone in need, for the sake of Jesus Christ our Lord. Amen.

Lord, you know the duties that lie before us this day;
the dangers that may confront us;
the temptations that may surround us.
Guide us, strengthen us, protect us;
for your dear Name's sake. Amen.

God, give me grace this day to stand for something,
lest I end up falling for anything. Amen.

Prayers in the Evening, at the End of the Day

It was a long but productive day, and we are ready to put our heads down on that pillow for some "snooze ops." Very ready. Few things are more appealing than well-deserved rest at the end of a hard workday. But before that, let me spend a minute or two with you, Lord.

Let me talk for a while, and then I will listen for you all night long.

Keep watch, dear Lord,
with those who work, or watch, or weep this night,
and give your angels charge over those who sleep.
Tend the sick, Lord Christ;
give rest to the weary;
bless the dying;
soothe the suffering;
pity the afflicted;
shield the joyous;
and all for your love's sake. Amen.

AT OTHER TIMES
OF THE DAY

A Song of Comfort for Difficult Times

> *Every year on Labor Day weekend, the Muscular
> Dystrophy telethon ends with host Jerry Lewis singing,
> "You'll Never Walk Alone." This song has warmed
> hearts for generations, and it has given strength and
> encouragement to countless people in troubled times
> and fearful nights.*

When you walk through a storm,
Hold your head up high
And don't be afraid of the dark.
At the end of the storm
Is a golden sky
And the sweet, silver song of a lark.
Walk on through the wind,
Walk on through the rain,
Though your dreams be tossed and blown.
Walk on, walk on with hope in your heart,
And you'll never walk alone!
You'll never walk alone.

God our Father,
we thank you for this day that is passing from us
    now.
For any glimpse of beauty we have seen;
for any echo of your truth we have heard;
for any kindness which we may have received;
for any good we may have been enabled to do;

and for any temptation which you gave us the
grace to overcome.
We thank you, O God; through Jesus Christ
our Lord.

O Lord God Almighty,
as you have taught us to call the evening,
the morning, and the noonday one day;
and have made the sun to know its going down:
Dispel the darkness of our hearts,
that by your brightness we may know you
to be the true God and eternal light,
living and reigning forever and ever. Amen.

For Saturday evening,
when Holy Communion follows on Sunday

As watchmen look for the morning, so do we look to
you, Lord Christ. Come with the dawning day and
make yourself known to us in your Holy Sacrament;
for you are our God forever and ever. Amen.

For Saturday evening,
when no Holy Communion follows on Sunday

O God, the source of eternal light:
shed forth your unending day upon us who watch
    for you,
that our lips may praise you,
our lives may bless you,
and our worship on the morrow give you glory;
through Jesus Christ our Lord. Amen.

At the End of Any Day

Lord, give us expectant hearts whenever we pray,
so that we can receive that for which we pray—and
then get on with our work. Correct our careless and
sullen attitudes; help us to work with enthusiasm
and determination. Create in us clean hearts, O
God: put a new spirit in us. As this day ends, let its
successes be remembered and its disappointments
be forgotten. Then as part of our refresher training,
give us refreshing rest. Amen.

Generous God, we begin our prayer
and end this day in gratitude:
for a life of variety and possibility;
for a soul of sensitivity and searching;
for friends of objectivity and depth;
for opportunities that broaden and deepen;
for loved ones that require and inspire;
for challenges that search and test.
Each day you give us is full of potentials and options,
may we never waste what you have given.
It was all very plain to us today–and glorious. Amen.

Lord God of our fathers:
In the beginning you created the human race
to live in peace, but not complacency;
to be strong, but not arrogant;
to have convictions, but to be understanding of
     others;
to be sufficiently humble, not to be jealous of others.
Give us tonight and in the days ahead the grace to
live in the spirit of our creation. And always our
prayer is that, as those on duty stand watch tonight,
you continue to watch over us and those we love at
home. Amen.

Lord, we know there is only one life given to each of us. We pass by this way just once—this command, this billet, these people—and then we move on a little better or a little worse. We want to be able to look back on our lives and know that our passing by has made a difference—that we've given more than we've taken, that we've helped more that we've hurt. Guide us then as we try to live our lives well. Fill our days and nights with meaning and hope as we work and rest in your care. Amen.

Dear God in heaven, we want to thank you for having been with us today and for helping us. Continue to guard us through the night. Problems come to us in all sizes, but the biggest one that just keeps coming back from time to time is our own anxiety. It's that feeling inside that makes us irritable, restless, and discontented. And it doesn't feel good. Lord, melt away our worries and let this prayer give me a gentle nudge, a reminder that the world doesn't revolve around me. Things just tend to go better when we realize this. Give us safe passage this night. Amen.

Lord, you know us inside and out,
Through and through,
Everything we do,
Every thought,
Every step,
Every plan,
Every word.
You know our past and our future;
Your presence covers our every move;
Your knowledge of us sometimes comforts us:
Sometimes frightens us.
Tonight again, we place all that we are in your
    hands. Amen.

Talking to you, Lord . . . is easy . . . listening is
    what's really hard!
My mind gets cluttered up with noise and
    confusion and activity. . . .
I shut you out . . . or turn you off . . . or fill my
    mind with other thoughts to keep it busy.
Maybe I'm just afraid of what I am likely
    to hear . . . tonight.

Lord . . . slow me down . . . make me quiet . . .
shut out all sounds and distractions and speak
to me directly, Lord.
Speak and let me listen.
Then settle my mind and grant me restful sleep.
Amen.

O Lord, from the evening shadows we call your name. Into your hands we commit ourselves and seek your mercy and peace. Help us to recognize your grace that enables us to complete and make sense of what we started at morning light. Heal us from sin-made wounds. Assure us of your pardon and comfort us with your Word. Bring us through the night rested and refreshed. Amen.

O Lord, each of us has fears that betray; worries that capture and shake out our joy. We find ourselves in limbo because we are neither here nor there. We are in a time of transition, of getting ready. Change and chance surround us. Help us,

O Lord, to return to your presence. Show us the point and purpose of each day. All we ask is that you keep us on our feet so that we might walk with you. Bless us this night and grant us rest. Amen.

Eternal God, in stillness and reflection, we ponder the words of those who have spoken to us today, voices that echo messages we need to hear, telling us who they are, sharing with us who they believe we are. These are the relationships through whom your Spirit breathes and through whom our gratitude rises.
Bless those who:
laugh, lift and cheer us;
lead, and direct us;
disagree, challenge and question us;
prod, encourage and move us;
love, respect and need us;
care, sacrifice and touch us;
listen, pray and teach us. Amen.

Mighty God of life and hope, we are grateful for
    those special experiences which lift us above
    the mundane and the trivial:
for those sudden insights about the meaning of
    things;
for the courage to pick ourselves up again after a fall;
for our conviction that life must go on despite bad
    news from time to time;
for those bursts of energy that enable us to finish
    the tasks that once seemed impossible;
for solutions which come in the middle of the night;
for those beautiful moments with family and friends.
We end this day in thanks to you for all these
    times and more. Amen.

Heavenly Father, we give you thanks for a busy day.
There is always a lot for all of us to do each day, and
that helps make it go by fast. Fortunately it has not
gone by too fast for us to stop and pray and give
over to you the worries and concerns that can make
our day just too much to handle. Give us now rest,
and make us content, knowing we've done what we
could, where we could. Amen.

We thank you, Heavenly Father, that you have graciously kept us this day and we pray that you keep us this night from all harm and danger, that all our doings in life may please you. For into your hands we commend ourselves, our bodies, our souls, and all things. Let your holy angels be with us that no evil may come our way. Thank you for a safe week. Give us continued success in the tasks ahead. This we ask according to your will. Amen.

God, our Father in heaven, you have invited us to make room in our day for a moment like this. A moment where our thoughts, our wants, our wishes can be boldly spoken directly to you. For those times today that were low spots, we can now confidently find relief and cast our cares on you. For those moments that were good, that made us laugh, or feel appreciated and worthy, we thank you and look forward to tomorrow and the opportunity to be helpful to one another. Be with us this night and bless us in all we think, say and do. Amen.

Adjusting to Deployment

THIS IS THE HARDEST THING
YOU HAVE EVER DONE

Signing that enlistment contract took you away from what is safe and familiar, and it may put you in combat someday. Who are you, and what are you becoming? Is this what you want? Is it what God wants of you?

God wanted significant service from Jeremiah, so he prepared Jeremiah from before birth and promised to equip him for service in demanding situations yet to come. If you pay attention, you will find what God has sent you out to do, too.

This period of service is the hardest thing you have ever done or attempted to do. It may also be the most significant thing you will do in your whole life.

The Call of Jeremiah
Jeremiah 1:4–8

Now the word of the Lord came to me saying, "Before I formed you in the womb I knew you, and before you were born I consecrated you; I appointed you a prophet to the nations." Then I said, "Ah, Lord God! Truly I do not know how to speak, for I am only a boy." But the Lord said to me, "Do not say, 'I am only a boy'; for you shall go to all to whom I send you, and you shall speak whatever I command you. Do not be afraid of them, for I am with you to deliver you, says the Lord."

Psalm 101

I will sing of mercy and justice; *
　　to you, O Lord, will I sing praises.

I will strive to follow a blameless course;
oh, when will you come to me? *
　　I will walk with sincerity of heart within my house.

I will set no worthless thing before my eyes; *
　　I hate the doers of evil deeds;
　　they shall not remain with me.

A crooked heart shall be far from me; *
    I will not know evil.

Those who in secret slander their neighbors
       I will destroy; *
    those who have a haughty look and a proud
       heart I cannot abide.

My eyes are upon the faithful in the land,
       that they may dwell with me, *
    and only those who lead a blameless life shall
       be my servants.

Those who act deceitfully shall not dwell
       in my house, *
    and those who tell lies shall not continue
       in my sight.

I will soon destroy all the wicked in the land, *
    that I may root out all evildoers from the city
       of the Lord.

    Dear heavenly Father, there are always questions on our minds, questions about what we do, who we are, where our lives are going. That's a fact with which we live. What's hard to live with is that there aren't always ready answers to our questions.

And so we wrestle with frustration, anger, impatience or disappointment. Somewhere under all the questions lies one basic question: Do you care? And the answer is always a simple, uncomplicated Yes, you care. Help us to understand our questions, because they're good ones. And to accept your answers, because they're good for us. Amen.

Heavenly Father, look down on us this night and give us your peace. One of the hardest things for us to do is wait. Being patient just doesn't come naturally. To even practice patience we have to be right in the middle of a trying situation. But that's our prayer tonight, Lord, that you bless us with the gift of patience. Help us to be still and know that you are God. Whether at work or at rest tonight, quiet our souls so that our anticipation may be channeled in productive and positive ways, ways which represent the best of what you have created us to be. We commend our bodies and souls into your hands. Amen.

We who live with the reality of war, who must be the first to go in harm's way into battle, we pray that we might not have to use our power with a vengeance. Rather, Lord, we ask you to help the people of our world overcome their fears and mistrusts. Enable them to speak and comprehend one another, enough to reach an understanding whereby all of us might enjoy the treasure which surpasses all other treasures. Amen.

O God, before whose face the generations of humanity rise and pass away, you are the strength of those who suffer, and the destiny of those who die. Accept our stuttering prayers. Grant that we may perceive and know what things to do—and receive grace and power to fulfill what is expected of us. We commit our best efforts into your hands for safekeeping. Amen.

Mighty God, so much can happen in a day.
So many perplexing questions jump before us.
We wonder:
who will we meet,
what news can affect us deeply,
what problem or temptation may reoccur,
what burden will we need to bear
or what challenge will inspire us?

In all of these questions,
we humbly ask that
whatever the answers are, keep us from:
parking by our failures,
sulking with our ills,
flaunting our achievements,
missing the simplicity of our friendships,
and bartering our souls
for cheap solutions to difficult problems.
We pray in the name of one who is God
over all things, great and small. Amen.

WONDERING WHO YOU ARE

Sometimes I wonder who I am anymore, but you know . . .

Never underestimate the power of that magic-yet-terrifying time of turning eighteen years of age, leaving home, and wondering whether you can survive becoming an adult. This is clearly the hardest thing you have ever done.

Leaving the familiarity and safety of home and family and going farther away than you have ever been before can leave you feeling alone and without roots. You now stand in the tradition of Abraham, who set out on a journey at God's call with his whole household to an unknown destination with uncertain logistics and no plan to return home again. It is easier for you: you will return home eventually. Logisticians are planning for everything, but the greatest logistics element of all is the faithfulness of God who will accompany you wherever this deployment takes you and the promise of Jesus to be with us to the very end of the age. Love and faithfulness surround you.

The Old Mariner stopped to enjoy the majestic sunset that only sailors ever see. It was the kind of sunset that makes poets out of the rudest and crudest of us. An especially thankful emotion arose in the

Old Mariner who was overheard to say:
O My Dear God:
I know I ain't what I'm supposed to be,
And I know I ain't what I'm going to be,
But thank you that I ain't what I used to be!

Psalm 139:1–9, 22–23

Lord, you have searched me out and known me; *
    you know my sitting down and my rising up;
    you discern my thoughts from afar.

You trace my journeys and my resting-places *
    and are acquainted with all my ways.

Indeed, there is not a word on my lips, *
    but you, O Lord, know it altogether.

You press upon me behind and before *
    and lay your hand upon me.

Such knowledge is too wonderful for me; *
    it is so high that I cannot attain to it.

Where can I go then from your Spirit? *
    where can I flee from your presence?

If I climb up to heaven, you are there; *
    if I make the grave my bed, you are there also.

If I take the wings of the morning *
    and dwell in the uttermost parts of the sea,

Even there your hand will lead me *
    and your right hand hold me fast.

Search me out, O God, and know my heart; *
    try me and know my restless thoughts.

Look well whether there be any wickedness in me *
    and lead me in the way that is everlasting.

Psalm 15

Lord, who may dwell in your tabernacle? *
    who may abide upon your holy hill?

Whoever leads a blameless life and does
            what is right, *
    who speaks the truth from his heart.

There is no guile upon his tongue;
he does no evil to his friend; *
    he does not heap contempt upon his neighbor.

In his sight the wicked is rejected, *
    but he honors those who fear the Lord.

He has sworn to do no wrong *
    and does not take back his word.

He does not give his money in hope of gain, *
  nor does he take a bribe against the innocent.
Whoever does these things *
  shall never be overthrown.

It's lonely out here, Lord. Although there are hundreds of other people very close by, sometimes I feel alone. Maybe I'm really missing that one special person back home. Perhaps it's the vast emptiness out here that makes me seem so small and isolated. Or it could be that the pressures of the day have seemed to close in on me, cutting me off from other people. Whatever it is, Lord, it's a lonely feeling. Thanks for being here with me, and thanks for listening. Amen.

As we gaze out at the vast expanse of the world, created by your hand, O God, we acknowledge your greatness. Who are we, Father, that you have reached out to us in loving kindness? Who are we, indeed, but your people, your children, the sheep of your pasture. Thank you for being our kind and

loving Shepherd, whom we know we can trust to be
with us through the night. Amen.

I asked for strength that I might achieve;
You made me weak that I might obey.
I asked for health that I might do greater things;
You gave me grace that I might do better things.
I asked for riches that I might be happy;
You gave me poverty that I might be wise.
I asked for power that I might have the praise of
    others;
You gave me weakness that I might feel the need
    of God.
I asked for all things that I might enjoy life;
You gave me life that I might enjoy all things and
    be thankful.
I received nothing that I asked for, but all that I
    hoped for,
My prayer was answered, and I was blessed.
    Amen.

O God, in a world that loves but little and distrusts in megatons, we need more evidence of your sustaining presence, your promise of peace. Cynical people continue to point out the many wooly-clad wolves that roam about. Help what we do to be more than a gesture, O Lord. Affirm us as we stand our ground and thus sacrifice our safety so that others can be provided a forum for their separate needs. Allow our courage in the face of constant threat to bring hope to this troubled land. Peace remains a slippery and elusive affair, O Lord. We can't quite make it on our own, so we entrust ourselves and our country's cause to you. Amen.

SEARCHING FOR GOOD WISDOM

Lord, I am searching for good wisdom. Have you some for me?

Everybody is so focused on what you and your unit have come here to do. You really do need to pay attention, because this work can get dangerous fast. Still, there are moments to ourselves and we search to see the larger picture of God's wisdom and hand active in the world. Alcoholics Anonymous and the other twelve-step programs have something called the "Serenity Prayer," and members carry a pocket coin with the Serenity Prayer text printed on it to help them remember what is important and to endure hard times. We start by going to the source of that prayer. The first prayer in this section is attributed to Reinhold Niebuhr.

God grant us serenity to accept the things we cannot change, courage to change the things we can and the wisdom to know the difference; living one day at a time; enjoying one moment at a time; accepting hardship as a pathway to peace taking this sinful world as it is, not as we would have it; so that we may be reasonably happy in this life and supremely happy with you forever in the next. Amen.

Psalm 1

Happy are they who have not walked in the
        counsel of the wicked, *
    nor lingered in the way of sinners,
    nor sat in the seats of the scornful!

Their delight is in the law of the Lord, *
    and they meditate on his law day and night.

They are like trees planted by streams of water,
bearing fruit in due season, with leaves that do
        not wither; *
    everything they do shall prosper.

It is not so with the wicked; *
    they are like chaff which the wind blows away.

Therefore the wicked shall not stand upright when
        judgment comes, *
    nor the sinner in the council of the righteous.

For the Lord knows the way of the righteous, *
    but the way of the wicked is doomed.

Lord, a wise man once said:
"Watch your thoughts, they become words;
watch your words, they become actions;
watch your actions, they become habits;
watch your habits, they become character;
watch your character, for it becomes your destiny."
Good Lord, help me watch more closely. Amen.

Psalm 101

I will sing of mercy and justice; *
    to you, O Lord, will I sing praises.

I will strive to follow a blameless course;
oh, when will you come to me? *
    I will walk with sincerity of heart within
        my house.

I will set no worthless thing before my eyes; *
    I hate the doers of evil deeds;
    they shall not remain with me.

A crooked heart shall be far from me; *
    I will not know evil.

Those who in secret slander their neighbors
        I will destroy; *

those who have a haughty look and a proud
        heart I cannot abide.
My eyes are upon the faithful in the land,
        that they may dwell with me, *
    and only those who lead a blameless life shall
        be my servants.
Those who act deceitfully shall not dwell in
        my house, *
    and those who tell lies shall not continue in
        my sight.
I will soon destroy all the wicked in the land, *
    that I may root out all evildoers from the city
        of the Lord.

Lord, what do we do about these decisions we
have to make? As you must surely know, they are not
always easy. We've heard people tell us before that
you will help us with decisions, so show us a way,
give us an answer. Lord, help us to believe that you
know our troubles, that you do help us. Don't let
us be blind to your direction, it may come in words
or the concern of a friend, or it may come from

within our own spirit and conscience. Most of all, let us make our decisions with peace of mind and firm trust that our lives are in your care. Amen.

Heavenly Father, there's probably a lot of times when our prayers sound like this: "Lord, make things go the way I want them to go." Help us, Lord, to trust that a prayer like that is a good prayer, because it strengthens our hope and recalibrates our plans. But, if you have something else planned for us, if the way we want things to go isn't necessarily the way that will best benefit us or those around us, help us to match prayer for prayer, our desires with the prayer you taught us, "Thy Will be done." Amen.

O Almighty and everlasting God, creator of heaven, earth and the universe, help me to be, to think, to act what is right because it is right; make me truthful, honest, and honorable in all things; make me stand up for the sake of right and honor and without thought of reward. Give me the ability to be kind, forgiving and patient with those around me. Help me to understand their motives and their shortcomings—even as you understand mine. In your most holy Name we commend them. Amen.

Lord God, before we ask you to take our whole lives into your keeping, just give us enough faith to live with you the very next moment—and then the next, and the next.

Before we ask you to build up our confidence in the whole human race, just give us enough courage to trust the next man we meet—and then the next, and the next.

Before we ask you to make a complete success in our entire life's work, just help us put our honor into the next task we undertake—and then the next, and the next.

Before we ask you to make us popular or esteemed by all men, just help us mirror your way of life the next time someone takes a look at us—and then the next, and the next.

Before we ask you to make us complete masters of our fate, just help us handle the next situation we face—and then the next, and the next. Amen.

Most Holy Father, may all voices be still except your own. Speak slowly and plainly to us, for we are slow to hear your voice and we are not wise enough to discern spiritual things readily or accurately.

Bring quiet to our anxious hearts and minds. Keep us from following after transient and alluring pleasures that do not yield lasting satisfaction.

We bring ourselves to you as we are and where we are. Have mercy on us. Create us anew, and then let us move again among our comrades as pilgrims who have been remade by your act of love. Amen.

Eternal Father, ruler and guardian of our lives, we
    beseech you to turn our sadness into joy and
    our failures into success.
By the discipline of duty, teach us self-control.
By the lessons of frustrated love, guide us to holier
    relationships with others.
By the insight of loss and sorrow, open to us the
    doors of understanding.
By the gall of pin-pricked pride, drive us to truer,
    humbler estimates of ourselves.
In the spotlight of reason, drive us to think more
    nearly as we ought.

Father, take the miseries of our lives and create
   from them your divine and holy mercies.
That we may find in each morning a day's dawn
   for service and a day's time for our souls to
   grow. Amen.

Sometimes, Lord, my ambition exceeds my effort . . .
I want to know without learning . . .
I act without thinking . . .
I want to have without trying . . .
Time runs out and I am left with little. . .
I must begin again . . . patience and perseverance . . .
How badly I need those two things . . . but why
   tell you, Lord?
You know me better than I know myself . . . but,
   it feels better Lord, just telling you anyway.
   Help me, Lord. Amen.

Lord of life,
We love you, but not enough.
We look for you, but don't spend much effort.
We listen for you, but make a lot of noise
    ourselves at the same time.
We try to understand, if it doesn't change us more
    than we like.
Lord of life, draw us closer to yourself.
When we find we are wrong, make us willing to
    change;
and, when we are right, make us easy to live with.
    Amen.

Almighty God, all of us must cope with the contradiction of our calling. We live in separation from those we love so that a nation can live together in peace, and take it for granted. We cross the great expanses of the oceans, so others can cross the street in freedom and safety. We rehearse ourselves, daily, in the art of war so that others can enjoy the fruits of a peaceful security. Help us not to doubt ourselves or our special calling to serve. Raise us up to know fully of your faith in us, as we seek desperately to increase our faith in you. Amen.

One blessing understands how we wish to be seen by others; the other appreciates how we often see ourselves. Why we never lose sight of our need to be blessed and so in these private moments at the end of a public day we ask for your blessing, once again. Amen.

⁘

Such a Wide and Wondrous World

Recruiting Poster: "Join the Navy and See the World!"

One of the delightful experiences in uniform is to see all the wondrous places that others only read about and see in picture books at the library or on coffee tables. You have set out on a great adventure. You will see the wonders of God's creation and then see what man has done with it—and you will be amazed at both. Keep your camera handy!

Many ships deploying to the Mediterranean Sea stop at Naval Air Station ROTA in Spain's southwestern Costa de la Luz. Right across the harbor is Cadiz—traditionally identified as the biblical town of

Tarshish and the western end of the biblical world. From here to the east, you are in the land of the Bible, and a time of adventurous pilgrimage begins there and through the Strait of Gibraltar. The first prayer in this section is for your eastbound passage through the Strait and in anticipation of passing westward to go home in a few months.

Keep your appreciation of what you see close to your heart. Never forget that it all begins with what God has made. Whenever you see God's wonders around you, Psalm 8 is always an appropriate praise of thanks.

Psalm 8

O Lord our Governor, *
 how exalted is your Name in all the world!

Out of the mouths of infants and children *
 your majesty is praised above the heavens.

You have set up a stronghold against your
  adversaries, *
 to quell the enemy and the avenger.

When I consider your heavens, the work of
  your fingers, *
 the moon and the stars you have set in
  their courses,

What is man that you should be mindful of him? *
    the son of man that you should seek him out?

You have made him but little lower than the angels; *
    you adorn him with glory and honor;

You give him mastery over the works of your hands; *
    you put all things under his feet:

All sheep and oxen, *
    even the wild beasts of the field,

The birds of the air, the fish of the sea, *
    and whatsoever walks in the paths of the sea.

O Lord our Governor, *
    how exalted is your Name in all the world!

O Lord, as the majestic gates of Africa and Europe seemed to unfold before us this day, we began a new chapter in our present history. What a fine preface! The air was mellow and clear, and for at least a while, we felt relaxed and refreshed again. O Lord, what a beautiful world you have made!

As we transit this sea, O God, help us to remember that on these shores that create our horizon we trace the borders of our spiritual home and history. Help us to be true to the Covenant you have written on our hearts and woven into the fabric of that which is good and of value in our civilization. O Lord, when to starboard we again pass Gibraltar's stark face, allow us to clear that portal with clear conscience and thankful hearts, for you are our guide and protector, a just and living God. Bless us on our journey and grant us a peaceful night. Amen.

Timeless God, for us who go to sea, the dimension of time seems often an enemy, separating us from loved ones; and other times it appears a friend. Teach us that time is neither friend nor foe—every minute starts an hour, and what one day may take from us, another day gives back. The Apostle Paul encourages us to redeem the time—perhaps he meant for us to enjoy the present hour, be thankful for the past, and order our lives in such a way that the gift of today will become our achievement for tomorrow, for you give us our future one day at a time. May we be worthy of all of its possibilities, its surprises and its fulfillment. Amen.

We thank you for the toughening experiences of life which signal not only the outward movement of our ship—but the upward movement of our lives, en route to actions which count for something. Bless our journey, O God, which fills us and fulfills us; and bless those who await our return. Amen.

Heavenly Father, thank you for bringing us safely across the line of the Equator. Though it certainly was a busy day, one that took a lot of effort, when you get down to it, today just wasn't that complex. Simply put we got dirty—then we got clean. I don't think I've ever been so thankful for soap and water. Thanks for soap and water and its ability to remove the foul and filth and replace it with the fresh fragrance. Just as soap and water squares us away on the outside, may we be squared away on the inside with pride for the ability you've given all of us to walk, upright, heads held high in service to you and our country. Amen.

❦

Eternal God, we look forward to liberty with memories to be made of exotic food and friendly people and historic places. Those were new and exciting places for many of us—part of the adventure we signed up for. Now we have another opportunity to be proud of our country and increase goodwill for her, to stir new respect and positive feelings for our nation. This remarkable crew has already an enviable reputation. May it become even better. Let each one of us enjoy the pleasures of this liberty. Let the memories we take with us be as satisfying as the experiences themselves. Make us proud of one another when we weigh anchor. Let neither carelessness nor callousness blind us to the privileged responsibilities we have to ourselves, to those we love, and to our shipmates. Amen.

❦

O Lord, help us to be in touch with the pulse-beat of the proud people who we will meet in this place we have never visited before—at times poor, but rich in a sense of history and the deep and abiding values of their ancient, yet viable cultures. As we will find, O Lord, families wear many faces and yet share together a growing need to interact with common purpose. O God of us and them, let us use this time to gather and treasure those events and scenes which make life so inviting and real. Be with us this night. Amen.

PLEASANT TIMES TOGETHER

Sometimes the days are just so special. We are far away from home with people we never would have met otherwise; yet we are doing some wonderful things that would never happen in our hometowns. These are the times we will remember when all the hard times are gone. These are the times we will remember in telling stories to our friends in years to come.

Lord, we'd like to thank you for the popcorn. That's right, nice, ordinary salted, hot buttered popcorn. I bet a lot of us popcorn lovers forget to thank you for such trivial things as popcorn. So this prayer is dedicated to trivial things like popcorn. What would a movie be without popcorn? Nothing. A good movie becomes a great movie when popcorn is served. So thanks for the popcorn, Lord. If you think enough of us to give us the little things like popcorn, you must think enough of us to give us the essential needs too. I pray that I always think enough of you to thank you for popcorn. Amen.

Now I lay me down to sleep,
I pray you Lord my soul to keep;
Grant no other sailor take
my shoes and socks before I wake.
Keep me safely in your sight,
and grant no GQ drill tonight.
In the morning let me wake
breathing scents of sirloin steak.
Lord, protect me in my dreams,
and make this better than it . . . seems. Amen.

O Lord our God, we confess that in dealings with each other we often are like a clam—98 percent mouth and covered with a hard shell. A friend has a problem and rather than listen, we sound off. A job doesn't go quite right and rather than learn, we spout off. Lord, you made us with two ears for every mouth. Help us to take this hint from your creation. Make us slow to speak and ready to listen, that we may better understand and pull together to get the job done and safely home again. Amen.

Our Heavenly Father, I watched a friend putting together a puzzle today. Carefully he examined each piece and first put together the outline. As the pieces filled in the center, the beautiful picture began to take form. Help us to discover the outline of our life, that we may discover the beautiful picture you have designed for us as the pieces come together. Sometimes the pieces didn't fit; carefully my friend replaced them with other pieces; but he didn't throw the others away.

Help us to recognize those pieces of our life that don't fit because we have made wrong choices; grant us grace to carefully select others that do.

The puzzle wasn't finished when I left; there were pieces yet to be placed.

O Father in Heaven, tonight we commend to your care the unfinished puzzles of our lives; trusting only in your goodness and your love to finish us as you would have us to be. Amen.

Lord, tonight peace reigns once again here. Our tired and sore bodies need their rest. Help us to use these quieter times to reflect on our lives— not just the events of recent hours, but also the adventures that await us in the days and months ahead. Help us to use our time profitably, as people who are thoughtful about their lives, their goals, and their ambitions. Raise our sights to find noble purposes that benefit us and those we love, for whom we also pray tonight. Amen.

Lord, taps reminds us that another period of time has passed. Everywhere else there is morning and evening, day and night, work and rest. Taps is a momentary pause when we are called to prayer. In the hectic pace of our lives, we are grateful for this quiet time, when we are reminded of whom and whose we are. Bless us tonight and fill the hectic hours of our life with meaning and hope, as we work and rest in your care. Amen.

"O God, our help in ages past, our hope for years to come; our shelter from the stormy blast, and our eternal home." We thank you, Lord, for a warm, dry place to sleep, for abundant good food to take away our hunger, for friends whose presence helps to ease the boredom of waiting for the unknown. We thank you, Lord, for the gift of life itself, and for the meaning and purpose that our faith in you brings to our lives. Give us now your peace. In your strong and powerful name we pray. Amen.

Dear God: Some days it's just a pleasure to be alive. Blue skies above and blue seas around. No pressing engagements. No last minute deadlines. Some time to play a little basketball or cards or just kick back and relax. For many of us today was that kind of day, and we enjoyed it. Thanks, Lord. Amen.

AWAY FROM HOME FOR THE HOLIDAYS

We sure do miss being home for the holidays. . . .

Serving far from home at Christmas is how most of us experience what it means to be away from home when we would rather be at home. It is a sign of growing up to be away from family and friends at the Christmas holidays, and it happens to everybody sooner or later. At least you are with friends and doing something important!

What follows is a collection of prayers for days that appear on the calendar and may be celebrated wherever you are. There are also some helpful resources, and the first one is that legendary answer to Virginia's question to the editor of the New York Sun *about whether there is a Santa Claus. If you visit Bari on the east coast of Italy, visit the Basilica of St. Nicholas where he is buried in the crypt below the main altar.*

Deployers keep count of their Christmases away from home. It is the hardest time to be away from family. Christmas can also be a special time to be deployed and to experience it in Israel or Vatican City, with host families overseas, and with your faith group's overseas congregations. Look around—there may be a very special opportunity awaiting you.

Yes, Virginia, There Is a Santa Claus
Editorial Page, *New York Sun*, 1897

We take pleasure in answering thus prominently the communication below, expressing at the same time our great gratification that its faithful author is numbered among the friends of *The Sun*:

"I am 8 years old. Some of my little friends say there is no Santa Claus. Papa says, 'If you see it in *The Sun*, it's so.' Please tell me the truth, is there a Santa Claus?" —Virginia O'Hanlon

Virginia, your little friends are wrong. They have been affected by the skepticism of a skeptical age. They do not believe except what they see. They think that nothing can be which is not comprehensible by their little minds. All minds, Virginia, whether they be men's or children's, are little. In this great universe of ours, man is a mere insect, an ant, in his intellect as compared with the boundless world about him, as measured by the intelligence capable of grasping the whole of truth and knowledge.

Yes, Virginia, there is a Santa Claus.

He exists as certainly as love and generosity and devotion exist, and you know that they abound and give to your life its highest beauty and joy. Alas! how dreary would be the world if there were no Santa Claus! It would be as dreary as if there were no Virginias. There would be no childlike faith then, no poetry, no romance to make tolerable this existence. We should have no enjoyment, except in sense and sight. The external light with which childhood fills the world would be extinguished.

Not believe in Santa Claus! You might as well not believe in fairies. You might get your papa to hire men to watch in all the chimneys on Christmas Eve to catch Santa Claus, but even if you did not see Santa Claus coming down, what would that prove? Nobody sees Santa Claus, but that is no sign that there is no Santa Claus. The most real things in the world are those that neither children nor men can see. Did you ever see fairies dancing on the lawn?

Of course not, but that's no proof that they are not there. Nobody can conceive or imagine all the wonders there are unseen and unseeable in the world.

You tear apart the baby's rattle and see what makes the noise inside, but there is a veil covering the unseen world which not the strongest man, nor even the united strength of all the strongest men that ever lived could tear apart. Only faith, poetry, love, romance, can push aside that curtain and view and picture the supernal beauty and glory beyond. Is it all real? Ah, Virginia, in all this world there is nothing else real and abiding.

No Santa Claus? Thank God he lives and lives forever. A thousand years from now, Virginia, nay 10 times 10,000 years from now, he will continue to make glad the heart of childhood.

Merry Christmas and a Happy New Year!!!!

The Nativity of Our Lord: Christmas Day
25 December

O God, you make us glad by the yearly festival of the birth of your only Son Jesus Christ: Grant that we, who joyfully receive him as our Redeemer, may with sure confidence behold him when he comes to be our Judge; who lives and reigns with you and the Holy Spirit, one God, now and for ever. Amen.

O God, you have caused this holy night to shine with the brightness of the true Light: Grant that we, who have known the mystery of that Light on earth, may also enjoy him perfectly in heaven; where with you and the Holy Spirit he lives and reigns, one God, in glory everlasting. Amen.

Almighty God, you have given your only-begotten Son to take our nature upon him, and to be born this day of a pure virgin: Grant that we, who have been born again and made your children by adoption and grace, may daily be renewed by your Holy Spirit; through our Lord Jesus Christ, to whom with you and the same Spirit be honor and glory, now and for ever. Amen.

Dr. Martin Luther King's Birthday
15 January

Lord, there are many who have gone before us who have made this world a better place for us. Today we remember the birth of such a man. We understand that you have so linked our lives with one another that all we do affects, for good or ill, all others. Martin Luther King, Jr., taught us that we are all your offspring—whether we are red or yellow, black or white, he encouraged us to live and work together in peace and challenged us to make the world a better place for all our sisters and brothers. We are the beneficiaries of his work and must continue to link our lives with one another, so that we too can provide freedom and justice for those who follow us. The task for which Dr. King gave his life must surely be our task. Amen.

Easter Day

O God, who for our redemption gave your only-begotten Son to the death of the cross, and by his glorious resurrection delivered us from the power of our enemy: Grant us so to die daily to sin, that we may evermore live with him in the joy of his resurrection; through Jesus Christ your Son our Lord, who lives and reigns with you and the Holy Spirit, one God, now and for ever. Amen.

O God, who made this most holy night to shine with the glory of the Lord's resurrection: Stir up in your Church that Spirit of adoption which is given to us in Baptism, that we, being renewed both in body and mind, may worship you in sincerity and truth; through Jesus Christ our Lord, who lives and reigns with you, in the unity of the Holy Spirit, one God, now and for ever. Amen.

Almighty God, who through your only-begotten Son Jesus Christ overcame death and opened to us the gate of everlasting life: Grant that we, who celebrate with joy the day of the Lord's resurrection, may be raised from the death of sin by your life-giving Spirit; through Jesus Christ our Lord, who lives and reigns with you and the Holy Spirit, one God, now and for ever. Amen.

Armed Forces Day
3rd Saturday in May

Lord, we're grateful for the good and gracious land in which we live, for the earth that is our home, and for the sea on which we practice our trade. On this Armed Forces Day we recall the courage and sacrifices of those who have gone before us, who have given great effort—and sometimes their lives—to secure our country's freedom. We are mindful of the price they paid to make life better for us. We continue their work proudly here, and we know just how much the American people are counting on us. Guide and preserve us and all who go in harm's way in search of lasting peace in our world and in our time, and bless our loved ones as well. Amen.

Memorial Day
30 May or the prior Monday

O Judge of the nations, we remember before you with grateful hearts the men and women of our country who in the day of decision ventured much for the liberties we now enjoy. Grant that we may not rest until all the people of this land share the benefits of true freedom and gladly accept its disciplines. This we ask in the Name of Jesus Christ our Lord. Amen.

Independence Day
4 July

Dear God of History, we return to sea, alive with fresh experiences of our national celebration. We have enjoyed the focus of a nation and its leaders. We have stood before a world as a symbol of continued vigilance, and now return to those efforts that require hard work and patience. But, let us always know that we exercise our duties before the one who seeks our face, and if a sparrow cannot fall to the ground without your notice, is it possible that an empire as great as ours can rise without your aid? Go with us as we learn that the liberty we celebrated this week does not stand without the responsible use of freedom. However difficult our future may be let our heritage be efforts to preserve freedom and extend it to all. Amen.

⁘

Lord God Almighty, in whose Name the founders of our country won liberty for themselves and for us, and lit the torch of freedom for nations then unborn: Grant that we and all the people of our land may have grace to maintain our liberties in righteousness and peace; through Jesus Christ our Lord, who lives and reigns with you and the Holy Spirit, one God, for ever and ever. Amen.

⁘

Labor Day
1st Monday in September

Lord, today could more appropriately be called Labor Month. The last few days have seemed a month long. It looks tonight that some can catch up on needed rest. We're grateful for that. As we quiet ourselves for rest, we remember those who stand the watches of the dark hours. Bless the hands on the helm, those who tend the engines below, who keep us on course, who repair or prepare. We can rest easy, knowing our comrades in arms are faithfully standing their watch. Bless their labors and bless the laborers of the night. Amen.

Thanksgiving Day
4th Thursday in November

Good and Gracious God, on this night before Thanksgiving it's very easy for us to conjure up memories of home and family and of course the feast that goes along with Thanksgiving Day. Lord, probably none of us can truly say we've ever known hunger. Surely not the hunger that would threaten our lives. And it's a fact we're well fed out here. We may not always like it but we have to admit there's plenty of food, and the cooks do their best to make it great. We thank you for all our food, Lord, whether it's bug-juice, or funny milk or peanut butter or steak and crab legs. Even the over-sized chickens that gobble instead of cluck we will share tomorrow, like all good things, come from you. Bless those folks in the Supply Department who work to procure and prepare turkey for all of us tomorrow. Bless us all out here and our families at home. Amen.

Lord God, heavenly Father, thank you for this special day, and for the special visitors we were privileged to host. Thank you for the growing pride we have in one another. Lord, give us the essentials: work to do, health, joy in simple things, an eye for beauty, a tongue for truth, a heart that loves, a mind that reasons, a sympathy that understands; give us neither malice nor envy, but a true kindness and plain old ordinary common sense. At the close of this day give us that peace that passes all understanding. We commend ourselves and all those dear to us to your strong care. Amen.

Heavenly Father, look down on us tonight and give us peace. We've come to the end of a week when thanksgiving was surely a focus. At times it seems that the days run into each other and we can begin to lose track of what day it is. So Lord, please help us to pause at the end of this week, and look forward to the next week with eagerness. Back home all of our folks and families will begin preparing for the season ahead. So will we. But more importantly help us to meet each day prepared to do the things we have to do. And if that's our prayer, Lord, we just can't sit around and wait. We have to be ready! Give us a ready attitude and ready responses that reflect a spirit ready to do what's right. Amen.

While On Duty

ALWAYS NEEDING TO BE READY

Some of our training is JIT training—just-in-time training, so that it will be fresh in our minds when we will need it soon, maybe even today.

Most of our training prepares us for what could happen at any time. They tell us that we may need to act someday in an emergency and that all this training will help us then. They are probably right: If we need to know how to do something right now, it is already too late to learn it—like in a fire or a crash. Readiness counts for a lot.

My personal protection equipment, my armor and my weapons, only do me some good when I have them on or ready to use. Most of it is defensive—for my own defense. I wear my belt, flack jacket, boots, shield, and helmet all the time if I could come under fire at any time. My only offensive weapon is ready at hand. Whatever comes and however suddenly it comes, I am ready to stand up under the assault.

St. Paul understands our situation, because he wrote about it:

Ephesians 6:10–18

Finally, be strong in the Lord and in the strength of his power. Put on the whole armor of God, so that you may be able to stand against the wiles of the devil. For our struggle is not against enemies of blood and flesh, but against the rulers, against the authorities, against the cosmic powers of this present darkness, against the spiritual forces of evil in the heavenly places. Therefore take up the whole armor of God, so that you may be able to withstand on that evil day, and having done everything, to stand firm. Stand therefore, and fasten the belt of truth around your waist, and put on the breastplate of righteousness. As shoes for your feet put on whatever will make you ready to proclaim the gospel of peace. With all of these, take the shield of faith, with which you will be able to quench all the flaming arrows of the evil one. Take the helmet of salvation, and the sword of the Spirit, which is the word of God. Pray in the Spirit at all times in every prayer and supplication. To that end keep alert and always persevere in supplication for all the saints.

⁂

Saint Patrick's Breastplate

> *St. Patrick's Breastplate is a poem of uncertain origin with a theme of binding to one's self the whole heritage and protection of God. The text below was adapted into a hymn lyric from the poem and presents a strong image of wearing God's protection as if it were body armor.*

Christ be with me, Christ within me,
Christ behind me, Christ before me,
Christ beside me, Christ to win me,
Christ to comfort and restore me.

Christ beneath me, Christ above me,
Christ in quiet, Christ in danger,
Christ in hearts of all that love me,
Christ in mouth of friend and stranger.

⁂

ASKING FOR GOD'S PROTECTION

*For maybe the first time in your life, you need more
protection than you can provide for yourself. Parents
and teachers are not around to protect you anymore.
Our country's enemies are now your own. All those
enemies that you used to just watch on television are
really there, and maybe they are not very far away.
Do you have some words of reassurance for us, Lord
God? Do you have some for me individually?*

Psalm 139:16–23

How deep I find your thoughts, O God! *
  how great is the sum of them!

If I were to count them, they would be more
      in number than the sand; *
  to count them all, my life span would need
      to be like yours.

Oh, that you would slay the wicked, O God! *
  You that thirst for blood, depart from me.

They speak despitefully against you; *
  your enemies take your Name in vain.

Do I not hate those, O Lord, who hate you? *
  and do I not loathe those who rise up against you?

I hate them with a perfect hatred; *
    they have become my own enemies.

Search me out, O God, and know my heart; *
    try me and know my restless thoughts.

Look well whether there be any wickedness in me *
    and lead me in the way that is everlasting.

Psalm 46:1–8

God is our refuge and strength, *
    a very present help in trouble.

Therefore we will not fear, though the earth
        be moved, *
    and though the mountains be toppled into
        the depths of the sea;

Though its waters rage and foam, *
    and though the mountains tremble at its tumult.

The Lord of hosts is with us; *
    the God of Jacob is our stronghold.

There is a river whose streams make glad the
        city of God, *
    the holy habitation of the Most High.
    God is in the midst of her;

she shall not be overthrown; *
    God shall help her at the break of day.

The nations make much ado, and the kingdoms
            are shaken; *
    God has spoken, and the earth shall melt away.

The Lord of hosts is with us; *
    the God of Jacob is our stronghold.

Psalm 23   (*King James Version*)

The Lord is my shepherd; *
    I shall not want.

He maketh me to lie down in green pastures: *
    he leadeth me beside the still waters.

He restoreth my soul: *
    he leadeth me in the paths of righteousness
            for his Name's sake.

Yea, though I walk through the valley of the
            shadow of death,
I will fear no evil: *
    for thou art with me;
    thy rod and thy staff, they comfort me.

Thou preparest a table before me in the presence
        of mine enemies: *
    thou anointest my head with oil;
    my cup runneth over.

Surely goodness and mercy shall follow me all
        the days of my life: *
    and I will dwell in the house of the Lord for ever.

Psalm 91

He who dwells in the shelter of the Most High, *
    abides under the shadow of the Almighty.

He shall say to the Lord,
"You are my refuge and my stronghold, *
    my God in whom I put my trust."

He shall deliver you from the snare of the hunter *
    and from the deadly pestilence.

He shall cover you with his pinions,
and you shall find refuge under his wings; *
    his faithfulness shall be a shield and buckler.

You shall not be afraid of any terror by night, *
    nor of the arrow that flies by day;

Of the plague that stalks in the darkness, *
    nor of the sickness that lays waste at mid-day.

A thousand shall fall at your side
and ten thousand at your right hand, *
    but it shall not come near you.

Your eyes have only to behold *
    to see the reward of the wicked.

Because you have made the Lord your refuge, *
    and the Most High your habitation,

There shall no evil happen to you, *
    neither shall any plague come near your dwelling.

For he shall give his angels charge over you, *
    to keep you in all your ways.

They shall bear you in their hands, *
    lest you dash your foot against a stone.

You shall tread upon the lion and adder; *
    you shall trample the young lion and the
            serpent under your feet.

Because he is bound to me in love,
therefore will I deliver him; *
    I will protect him, because he knows my Name.

He shall call upon me, and I will answer him; *
    I am with him in trouble;
    I will rescue him and bring him to honor.

With long life will I satisfy him, *
    and show him my salvation.

O God, before whose face the generations of
humanity rise and pass away, you are the strength
of those who suffer, and the destiny of those who
die. Accept our stuttering prayers. Grant that we
may perceive and know what things to do—and
receive grace and power to fulfill what is expected
of us. We commit our best efforts into your hands
for safekeeping. Amen.

Grant us safety, Lord, as we travel on our way.
With you began and with you shall end this day;
guard our lips from sin, our hearts from shame,
that on this deployment none may have called
upon your name except in faith. Grant us your
peace, Lord, through the coming night; turn for us
its darkness into light; from harm and danger keep
each of us free, for dark and light are both alike to
you. Amen.

O Lord, the sky and sea are hauntingly beautiful this evening, and yet the reality of the present is the stormy ocean about us that heaves and sighs and calls us to do its bidding. Help us to ride out the gale. It's exciting that you carry us in your loving hand. Most importantly, keep us from injury as we toss and turn in turbulent seas. Amen.

O Lord, ours is a mariner's prayer echoing through the centuries, but one which rings true— for the sea is the great humbler of the self-sufficient. Hear our simple prayer. Guard and protect our shipmates this night. Protect our families, and reassure them. Keep your Sabbath promise. Bring us rest. Amen.

We thank you, our Father, for the experiences of this day. You have been with us through the good as well as the not-so-good experiences. Thank you, Lord, for continuing to love us, even when we have not been altogether good or lovable. Be with us and with our families this night. Accompany those who will be on watch. And as the new day approaches, give us a renewed determination to do all things well and according to your will. Keep us safe, we pray, in your holy Name. Amen.

O Lord, you know well that it hasn't been easy to find you. Our faith has often slipped between the cracks. Reality has pressed us to the wall. And yet we conclude, O God, that even though it is often hard to believe, it is even harder not to believe. We need you as a son needs a father, a student a teacher, a friend a companion and a wanting person a savior. O Lord, we thank you for being with us, especially in the dangers that surround us. Help us to continue to approach you with confidence and prayer. Be with us and bless us, O Lord, as we begin a new day. Give us peace this night. Amen.

During a Quiet Watch

It sure is a quiet watch . . .

Sometimes it gets really quiet late at night, but we are standing watch alone in the dead of the night and expecting nothing special to happen. I sure hope it stays that way! And I wonder if anybody knows I am here and cares what I am doing. Whatever happens—or not—I need to stay awake and pay attention.

A friend who served in the 1991 Gulf War in Kuwait got it right: "Never let a quiet watch lull you into a false sense of security." I will stay alert, because others are depending on me. I will keep a prayer on my lips and a song in my heart. When somebody finally comes to relieve me, then I will get my rest—beautiful, blessed, and well-deserved rest.

Psalm 130:1–5

Out of the depths have I called you, O Lord;
Lord, hear my voice; *
> let your ears consider well the voice of
> > my supplication.

If you, Lord, were to note what is done amiss, *
> O Lord, who could stand?

For there is forgiveness with you; *
    therefore you shall be feared.

I will wait for the Lord; my soul waits for him; *
    in his word is my hope.

My soul waits for the Lord,
more than watchmen for the morning, *
    more than watchmen for the morning.

1 Peter 5:8–9

Discipline yourselves, keep alert. Like a roaring lion your adversary the devil prowls around, looking for someone to devour. Resist him, steadfast in your faith, for you know that your brothers and sisters in all the world are undergoing the same kinds of suffering.

Be present, O most merciful God, and protect us through the silent hours of this night, so that we who are wearied by the changes and chances of this fleeting world may rest upon thy eternal changelessness; through Jesus Christ our Lord. Amen.

Lighten our darkness we beseech thee, O Lord, and by thy great mercy defend us from all perils and dangers of this night; for the love of thy only Son, our Savior Jesus Christ. Amen.

~

O God, your unfailing providence sustains the world we live in and the life we live: Watch over those, both night and day, who work while others sleep, and grant that we may never forget that our common life depends upon each other's toil; through Jesus Christ our Lord. Amen.

~

O God, Our Help in Ages Past

Our God, our help in ages past,
Our hope for years to come,
Our shelter from the stormy blast,
And our eternal home.

A thousand ages in thy sight
Are like an evening gone;
Short as the watch that ends the night
Before the rising sun.

Our God, our help in ages past,
Our hope for years to come,
Be thou our guard while troubles last,
And our eternal home.

—Isaac Watts

Psalm 139:10–17

If I say, "Surely the darkness will cover me, *
    and the light around me turn to night,"

Darkness is not dark to you;
the night is as bright as the day; *
    darkness and light to you are both alike.

For you yourself created my inmost parts; *
    you knit me together in my mother's womb.

I will thank you because I am marvelously made; *
    your works are wonderful, and I know it well.

My body was not hidden from you, *
    while I was being made in secret
    and woven in the depths of the earth.

Your eyes beheld my limbs, yet unfinished in
          the womb;
all of them were written in your book; *
    they were fashioned day by day,
    when as yet there was none of them.
How deep I find your thoughts, O God! *
    how great is the sum of them!
If I were to count them, they would be more
          in number than the sand; *
    to count them all, my life span would need
          to be like yours.

          ⟋ · · ⟍

    Dear God, it's evening now. Around me some
of the lights are going out and silence prevails. In
other places there is still a lot of activity. My prayer
tonight is that whether we now are quiet or active
we use this time profitably, as individuals who are
thoughtful about their lives, their goals and their
ambitions. Keep us from groveling about in a mire of
despair, and help us raise our sights to finer things,
with a purpose that benefits us and those we protect. Again tonight we ask that as those of us who on
duty stand watch around this place, you continue to
watch over us and those we love at home. Amen.

Come into our hearts, O Lord, in the darkness of this evening, leave us not unprotected. May the light of this evening's moon, the twilight of ten thousand stars, and the silence of the night be again divinely armed. Continue, O Gracious Master, to execute your universal orders as our heavenly Captain, so that when the morning sun musters us to another plan of the day, may your will be done on earth as it is in heaven. Amen.

Lord God, as we quiet ourselves this night, we stop to remember those others who must also stand the duties of the dark hours. Bless the hands on the wheel, those who stand the evening watches, those who tend the engines below. We thank you for their faithfulness in keeping us safe. May each one of us, no matter what our job, feel a sense of contributing to the welfare of our shipmates. In their lonely hours may they talk to you. Amen.

Lord God, our heavenly Father, we are not the kind of people who like to dwell on our short-comings but all too often like haunting ghosts, our shortcomings dwell with us. If left to ourselves with the burden of mistakes we've made, we could very easily be lost, lost into many rationalizations or lost in despair. Help us to remember you are a God of forgiveness. Take away our selfishness, our guilt, and our worry over things that are beyond our control. Give us strength to apply our hearts and minds to the things at hand, personal and pro-fessional, knowing that you are with us through the night. Into your hands we commend our bodies and our souls. Amen.

Lord, tonight the fog horn calls us to vigilance as taps calls us to prayer. Alert in body, mind and spirit we are ensured of safety and reassured in our hope. Give us expectant hearts so that we can receive that for which we pray, and then get on with our work. Correct any careless or sullen attitude. Help us watch with enthusiasm and determination. Create in us clean hearts, O God: put a right spirit within us. Amen.

Visit this place, O Lord, and drive far from it all
   snares of the enemy;
let your holy angels dwell with us to preserve us
   in peace;
and let your blessing be upon us always;
through Jesus Christ our Lord. Amen.

Sustain my waking, Good Lord, and guard those
   who sleep;
that awake I may keep my watch faithfully,
and that later in my sleep I may rest in peace.

Expecting to See Action Soon

*Even the bravest of us, behind the bravado, suffers
many mixed emotions at the prospect of what is going
to happen soon. We know what it means to be drawn
to greatness by the significance of what we are about
to accomplish; yet, we are intimidated by it and
frightened by the danger. Beyond our own realities
and imaginings, we know how many at home worry
for our safety and pray for our safe return.*

Here are a few of the noble prayers and stories of those who went before us. They were not saints, but we can stand on their shoulders to see into the kingdom of God as well as into the immediate days ahead.

Admiral Lord Nelson, *praying before the Sea Battle of Trafalgar, 1805*

Admiral Horatio Lord Nelson wrote this prayer on the morning of 21 October 1805 at his cabin on board HMS Victory with the combined fleets of France and Spain in sight and combat about to begin. If you visit HMS Victory at Her Majesty's Naval Base at Portsmouth in England, you can see the round table with a medallion in the center where he wrote this prayer. Lord Nelson died that afternoon in the battle, but not before learning that he had won the great Battle of Trafalgar.

May The Great God, whom I worship,
grant to my Country
and for the benefit of Europe in general,
a great and glorious Victory;
and may no misconduct, in any one, tarnish it;
and may humanity after victory be the
     predominant feature in the British Fleet.
For myself individually,

I commit my life to Him who made me,
and may His blessing light upon my endeavours
for serving my country faithfully.
To Him I resign myself
and the just cause which is entrusted to me to
    defend.
Amen. Amen. Amen.

*King Henry V, speaking to his troops before the
Battle of Agincourt, 1415*

*King Henry V and his forces faced overwhelming
opposition at the Battle of Agincourt in France on
25 October 1415. The evening before, he gathered
his troops together to encourage them, and probably
to encourage himself as well, before the battle to come
the next day—the feast day of St. Crispian. Surely,
the casualties would be severe. The King's speech is
memorialized by William Shakespeare:*

This day is call'd the feast of Crispian:
He that outlives this day and comes safe home
Will stand a tip-toe when this day is named,
And rouse him at the name of Crispian.
He that shall live this day and see old age,

Will yearly on the vigil feast his neighbours,
And say, "To-morrow is Saint Crispian":
Then he will strip his sleeve and show his scars,
And say, "These wounds I had on Crispin's day."
Old men forget; yet all shall be forgot,
But he'll remember with advantages
What feats he did on that day: then shall our names,
Familiar in his mouth as household words,
Harry the King, Bedford and Exeter,
Warwick and Talbot, Salisbury and Gloucester,
Be in their flowing cups freshly remember'd.
This story shall the good man teach his son;
And Crispin Crispian shall ne'er go by,
From this day to the ending of the world,
But we in it shall be remembered;
We few, we happy few, we band of brothers;
For he to-day that sheds his blood with me
Shall be my brother, be he ne'er so vile,
This day shall gentle his condition:
And gentlemen in England now a-bed
Shall think themselves accursed they were not here,
And hold their manhoods cheap whiles any speaks
That fought with us upon Saint Crispin's day.

—*Henry V* Act 4, Scene 3

For our Defense

Almighty Lord God: be now and evermore our
    defense;
grant us victory and the humility to use it
    according to your will;
look in pity upon the wounded and prisoners;
cheer the anxious;
comfort the bereaved;
succour the dying;
have mercy on the fallen;
and hasten the time when war shall cease in all
    the world;
through Jesus Christ our Lord. Amen.

In Time of War

Eternal Lord God, watch over our President
and country at this time and grant us to do your
will on earth. Give your guidance to those who
bear command over us at sea, on land, or by air;
remember us your servants, together with all our
fellow Sailors, Soldiers, Marines, Airmen, and Coast
Guardsmen, and hold us in your safe keeping in
life or in death. Comfort the wounded, have mercy

on the fallen, calm the anxious, strengthen the bereaved, reassure our families at home, and give us
your peace again; through Jesus Christ our Lord.
Amen.

Psalm 10:1–12, 16–19

Why do you stand so far off, O Lord, *
   and hide yourself in time of trouble?

The wicked arrogantly persecute the poor, *
   but they are trapped in the schemes they have
   devised.

The wicked boast of their heart's desire; *
   the covetous curse and revile the Lord.

The wicked are so proud that they care not for God; *
   their only thought is, "God does not matter."

Their ways are devious at all times;
your judgments are far above out of their sight; *
   they defy all their enemies.

They say in their heart, "I shall not be shaken; *
   no harm shall happen to me ever."

Their mouth is full of cursing, deceit,
            and oppression; *
    under their tongue are mischief and wrong.

They lurk in ambush in public squares
and in secret places they murder the innocent; *
    they spy out the helpless.

They lie in wait, like a lion in a covert;
they lie in wait to seize upon the lowly; *
    they seize the lowly and drag them away in
            their net.

The innocent are broken and humbled before
            them; *
    the helpless fall before their power.

They say in their heart, "God has forgotten; *
    he hides his face; he will never notice."

Rise up, O Lord;
lift up your hand, O God; *
    do not forget the afflicted.

Break the power of the wicked and evil; *
    search out their wickedness until you find none.

The Lord is King for ever and ever; *
    the ungodly shall perish from his land.

The Lord will hear the desire of the humble; *
    you will strengthen their heart and your ears
        shall hear;
To give justice to the orphan and oppressed, *
    so that mere mortals may strike terror no more.

Psalm 11

In the Lord have I taken refuge; *
    how then can you say to me,
    "Fly away like a bird to the hilltop;
For see how the wicked bend the bow
and fit their arrows to the string, *
    to shoot from ambush at the true of heart.
When the foundations are being destroyed, *
    what can the righteous do?"
The Lord is in his holy temple; *
    the Lord's throne is in heaven.
His eyes behold the inhabited world; *
    his piercing eye weighs our worth.
The Lord weighs the righteous as well as
        the wicked, *
    but those who delight in violence he abhors.

Upon the wicked he shall rain coals of fire and
        burning sulphur; *
    a scorching wind shall be their lot.

For the Lord is righteous;
he delights in righteous deeds; *
    and the just shall see his face.

Psalm 45:1–8, 18

My heart is stirring with a noble song;
let me recite what I have fashioned for the king; *
    my tongue shall be the pen of a skilled writer.

You are the fairest of men; *
    grace flows from your lips,
    because God has blessed you for ever.

Strap your sword upon your thigh, O mighty
        warrior, *
    in your pride and in your majesty.

Ride out and conquer in the cause of truth *
    and for the sake of justice.

Your right hand will show you marvelous things; *
    your arrows are very sharp, O mighty warrior.

The peoples are falling at your feet, *
   and the king's enemies are losing heart.

Your throne, O God, endures for ever and ever, *
   a scepter of righteousness is the scepter of
         your kingdom;
   you love righteousness and hate iniquity.

Therefore God, your God, has anointed you *
   with the oil of gladness above your fellows.

I will make your name to be remembered
from one generation to another; *
   therefore nations will praise you for ever
         and ever."

AFTER SEEING ACTION

We saw action, and we are thankful it is over.

*Mixed feelings run wild after dangerous times. Every-
body who survived to engage the enemy another day is
glad they made it. Everybody is also heavily burdened
by the sights and sounds of the action they witnessed
and how they participated. What some call "the fog
of war" makes it difficult to know what was really*

happening, and that fog does not lift quickly when things quiet down.

We look for good news. If the incident was particularly bad, good news may be that somebody was only injured and hospitalized.

Over on the enemy side, we know that they are just people trying to make their way through the world and provide for their families and country. A friend from the Royal Navy told of watching an Argentine ship sink during the Falkland War of 1983—and how in watching it fall under the waves nobody was cheering. They knew what others would miss: that the only real difference between themselves and those on the sinking ship were the countries where their parents, wives, and children were living.

If you ever want to meet really committed peacemakers, look to those who know they may yet be called to pay the price for it.

Still, it is great to be alive and well after the action.

Almighty Father, who of your great goodness has saved us in the day of battle and delivered us out of the hand of our enemies, we thankfully acknowledge your great goodness. May your grace enable us truly to thank you, and to devote to your service the lives which you have spared. Because you have been our help, we therefore offer to you now in gratitude our rejoicing and our thanks, and we dedicate our lives to you and the service of others; through Jesus Christ our Lord. Amen.

Psalm 9:1–9, 15–20

I will give thanks to you, O Lord, with my whole
        heart; *
  I will tell of all your marvelous works.

I will be glad and rejoice in you; *
  I will sing to your Name, O Most High.

When my enemies are driven back, *
  they will stumble and perish at your presence.

For you have maintained my right and my cause; *
  you sit upon your throne judging right.

You have rebuked the ungodly and destroyed
        the wicked; *
  you have blotted out their name for ever and ever.

As for the enemy, they are finished, in perpetual
        ruin, *

their cities ploughed under, the memory
     of them perished;

But the Lord is enthroned for ever; *
    he has set up his throne for judgment.

It is he who rules the world with righteousness; *
    he judges the peoples with equity.

The Lord will be a refuge for the oppressed, *
    a refuge in time of trouble.

The ungodly have fallen into the pit they dug, *
    and in the snare they set is their own foot caught.

The Lord is known by his acts of justice; *
    the wicked are trapped in the works of their
     own hands.

The wicked shall be given over to the grave, *
    and also all the peoples that forget God.

For the needy shall not always be forgotten, *
    and the hope of the poor shall not perish for ever.

Rise up, O Lord, let not the ungodly have the
     upper hand; *
    let them be judged before you.

Put fear upon them, O Lord; *
    let the ungodly know they are but mortal.

Psalm 55:1–6, 10–11, 24–26

Hear my prayer, O God; *
    do not hide yourself from my petition.

Listen to me and answer me; *
    I have no peace, because of my cares.

I am shaken by the noise of the enemy *
    and by the pressure of the wicked;

For they have cast an evil spell upon me *
    and are set against me in fury.

My heart quakes within me, *
    and the terrors of death have fallen upon me.

Fear and trembling have come over me, *
    and horror overwhelms me.

Swallow them up, O Lord;
confound their speech; *
    for I have seen violence and strife in the city.

Day and night the watchmen make their rounds
        upon her walls, *
    but trouble and misery are in the midst of her.

Cast your burden upon the Lord,
and he will sustain you; *
    he will never let the righteous stumble.

For you will bring the bloodthirsty and deceitful *
  down to the pit of destruction, O God.

They shall not live out half their days, *
  but I will put my trust in you.

Remembering Those Who Have Died

This Profession of Arms is dangerous business, and no small number of those who served before us have fallen and died just doing their duties for their country. Our home communities do not teach us well about doing our duty and not counting the cost, so when that cost has to be paid we find ourselves unprepared.

Admiral Horatio Lord Nelson addressed his crew in his flagship HMS Victory *on the morning before the Battle of Trafalgar, 21 October 1805. Speaking plainly, he said and sent by signal flags to the other ships, "England expects every man to do his duty." Little did he realize that he would lead by example that day and die before sunset—yet having learned that he had won the sea battle.*

In battle or exercises, we may well lose our friends in arms. It is rightfully painful, especially if we witness it all. Whatever you do, talk with friends before you go to bed that day so that your burden is shared early. If your friends are suffering, give them all the listening time you can manage.

And pray with friends. Here are some helps.

The first prayer is very powerful and is used by British and Commonwealth forces. It is especially useful for Remembrance Day services on 11 November.

We remember before you, good Lord,
and entrust to your keeping,
those who have died in defense of justice and
    freedom.
They shall not grow old as we that are left grow old:
Age shall not weary them nor the years condemn;
At the going down of the sun and in the morning
We will remember them.

Almighty and eternal God, from whose love in Christ we cannot be parted even by death, hear our prayers and thanksgivings for those we remember today. Fulfill in them the purpose of your love and bring us, with them, to your eternal joy; through Jesus Christ our Lord. Amen.

Lord God of our fathers, we pledge ourselves to serve you and all mankind in the cause of peace. Guide us by your Spirit; give us wisdom; give us courage; give us hope; and keep us faithful, now and always. Amen.

As we pause to lift our hearts and minds in prayer, let us be mindful of those who have laid down their lives in the service of their country. Lord, we ask your strength, that we might dedicate ourselves to perfecting your kingdom of peace and justice among nations. Let us give thanks for the many blessings of freedom which we possess, purchased at the cost of many lives and sacrifices. Fill us with the courage to fulfill our tasks and in no way break faith with the fallen. We commend these fallen to your mercy and ask that you give them eternal rest. This we ask and pray in your name. Amen.

Families Bound
Together in Prayer

*It is a big world out there. Our families stay settled
and home, and our deployers go . . . wherever.*

*When heading out on deployment, we rarely know
exactly where we will go, how long we will stay there,
or even what the mission might become once we get
there. If we do not know, neither do our families. We
go for six months or a year, and real world events may
change the whole thing. Our families may well find
out what we are doing by seeing us do it on television
before our letters and e-mails reach them. Change
happens fast, and real world events include us who
are forward deployed.*

*How helpful it is to know that our families, friends,
and congregations remember to pray for us—by name
and by command. Let's remember to be thankful for*

their prayers, love, and confidence in us; then, let's remember to pray for them, too.

We have people at home who love us, count on us, and pray for our safe return. They only have a vague notion of where we really are and what we are doing right now. That may be just as well. We are counting on them, too. We see the same stars in the sky, and we are all concerned for each other. We sing and pray for those we love back home, and they sing and pray for us.

FOR MY FAMILY BACK AT HOME

Teach us, O Lord, to appreciate the little things which have touched our lives while deployed so far from home in these last months—routine duty, a game of cards, small talk with our friends here. May we live deeply, drinking of the fountains that are all about us. We thank you for the beauty of this night and the fellowship that we enjoy. Watch over our loved ones as we quiet ourselves for this last night away. Bless us with such a homecoming tomorrow that the loneliness of separation will be quickly changed into the joy of reunion. Amen.

Into your hands, Good Lord, I commend my family back at home, trusting in your good will and providence to protect and guide them through the events of the day. Surely you and I know better than they do what is happening with all of us serving together over here so far away—they may have a sense of it at home, but they probably do not know what I will actually do today. I do not know what they are doing at any given moment either, nor do I know what they are actually doing right now. And even so, it is the trust that sustains our household that makes it possible for me to do this work of mine where I must concentrate on these details in sure confidence that you are overseeing the details back at home. So I entrust all of us—and you do see all of us—into your caring hands, knowing that you do more for us than we ever realize. Amen.

More and more, O Lord, we find ourselves thinking home thoughts. Our growing sense of anticipation allows us to shorten the distances between ourselves and those we love and long for. In their own way, O Lord, these are days of sustained turmoil. Pushed down feelings have begun to surface and the closely guarded secret of my essential humanity is beginning to be made public. Laughter comes quickly and tempers flare. And yet, O Lord, as with anything in life, reality still impinges upon us. Time and space continue to hold us tightly and our sense of duty and fear of failure remain to fix the boundary of a day that begins well before breakfast and ends far beyond taps. In this time of change and transition from here to there, O Lord, be our rock and our shield. Carry us through so that we may bless your name, for you are El Shaddai—the unchanging, eternal one. Grant us rest this night out here and a peaceful night for my household back home. Amen.

Lord, we give thanks tonight for all those who have loved us and have shown us an example of faithful and godly living while we are away on our country's business. We are grateful for those who have shown kindness when things were tough, those who helped when we couldn't help ourselves, and those who loved us when we didn't feel lovable. As our thoughts turn more and more toward home and our families there, we pray especially for those

who have special anxieties about returning home.
Help each of us to use the days ahead to prepare
ourselves for homecoming. Amen.

⁂

God, our heavenly Father, we pray you to
watch in your loving care over our homes, families and friends so far away. Keep far from them
all harm and danger; may your presence always
be with them, and may they please be aware of it;
through Jesus Christ our Lord. Amen.

⁂

God, our heavenly Father, look in love upon
our families and friends so far away. Protect them
from any harm, comfort them in loneliness and
prosper them in all good things. Let no shadow
of doubt come between them and us to divide our
hearts, and in your own good time bring us back
home to them again; through Jesus Christ our
Lord. Amen.

⁂

WHEN SOMEBODY IS SICK OR INJURED AT HOME

Lord God, keep under your protection all those whom we love; watch over my loved one who may be sick or in trouble, and keep us linked through prayer with all who have a place in our hearts; through Jesus Christ our Lord. Amen.

FOR OUR FAMILY READINESS COORDINATOR

Almighty God, our heavenly Father, whose blessed Son shared at Nazareth the life of an earthly home: We beseech you to bless our homes and families, and to keep us in our going out and in our coming in. Grant us day by day your strength and protection while our deployers are far away, and let that self-giving person who has taken leadership here at the Base as our Family Readiness Coordinator be blessed with wisdom and energy to lead our gathered families during these difficult months. Watch over us in times of danger and necessity; fill our hearts when there is good news to share and when we prepare for our deployers to come home again; and unite us with each other in your great love; through the same Jesus Christ our Lord. Amen.

Families Praying Together

We thank you, good Lord, that you are in every place and that neither time nor space can separate us from you, and that the leader in our household who is absent for a time and deployed on our country's business is still present with you. Have in your keeping our beloved one from whom we are now separated, and grant that both they and we, by drawing nearer to you, may all be drawn nearer to one another through Jesus Christ our Lord. Amen.

Lord, our Father, watch over our deployed family member. May your fatherly care be the shield and buckler of this household, and the love of your dear Son preserve deployers from all evil, the guidance of your Holy Spirit keep them in the way that leads to eternal life; through Jesus Christ our Lord. Amen.

God, our heavenly Father, we pray you of your great goodness to watch over those whom we love who are so very far away and for so long. Shield them from harm, guide them through all difficulties, and strengthen them by our Holy Spirit; through Jesus Christ our Lord. Amen.

God, our heavenly Father, so fill our hearts with trust in you, that by day and by night we may, without fear, commit those who are dear to us to your never-failing love for this life and the life to come—and even right now, when we need to know it, for the rest of this deployment. Amen.

God our Father, whose Son Jesus Christ left the shelter of his home at Nazareth to pursue his life's work, be with us here and with the one who is deployed from this household in our times of family separation. Give us strength in loneliness or temptation, and grant that we may be worthy of the love so freely poured out upon us; through Jesus Christ our Lord. Amen.

O God, the Protector and Helper of all thy children, the Comfort and Stay of the solitary and those who are separated from those they love, we commit unto thee and thy fatherly keeping our loved ones in deployment, beseeching thee to grant unto them every good gift for the body and soul, and to unite us all, present and absent, in true faith and love; through Jesus Christ our Lord. Amen.

FOR MY FIANCÉ OR FIANCÉE

O God, our Father, we pray you to bless us who are preparing for marriage, and fill us with such love one toward another and abiding trust during this long time deployed and apart that we may live together in holy peace in this world, and in the world to come obtain life everlasting. And while we remain apart for these months by this seemingly endless deployment, may we also rejoice together in the anticipation of our future household where you will be honored in every way. Amen.

FOR MY SPOUSE

Almighty God, bless our command's families and especially my loving and loyal spouse, that we each may be to the other a strength in need and a wise counselor in difficulty; a source of comfort in sorrow, and a companion in every joy. So bind us together in your will that we may enter your kingdom, in which life is the fulfilling of the law; through Jesus Christ our Lord. Amen.

For My Children

God our Father, whose Son Jesus left the shelter and safety of his home at Nazareth to pursue his life's work, my life's work has taken me across the world to a place so far away where it is so hard to accomplish that part of my life's work that was left behind at home—the parenting of my wonderful children. Do set your presence in my household back home, and let your Holy Spirit so bless my spouse and children, that they may be led faithfully to holiness and wisdom and that they may prosper in my absence, growing daily in wisdom and stature until we are reunited soon and together give thanks to you. Amen.

When a Child Has Been Born during Deployment

Dear Heavenly Father, the leaders of my command came to me today with a message that a child joined my family today while I was way out here. What a wonderful event! And how I love that little baby that I have not met but will meet in your good time and at the end of my operational schedule. I will keep a copy of that message with me wherever I go until I see this little baby as a reminder that you have cared for all of us in these difficult days and will deliver us safely to each other one day soon. Amen.

For My Children
Who May Be Confirmed

God, our wise and loving father, make ready the hearts and minds of your servants and my children who are seeking to be strengthened by the gift of your Holy Spirit through the laying-on of hands in Confirmation, that, drawing near with penitent and faithful hearts, they may be filled with the power of this same Spirit; through Jesus Christ our Lord. Amen.

For My Mother

Lord Jesus, you have known a mother's love and tender care, and I know you will hear this prayer I make for my own mother. Protect her life, I pray, who gave the gift of life to me; and may she know from day to day, the deepening glow of joy that comes from you. I cannot pay my debt for all the love that she has given me; but you, Lord, will not forget her due reward. Bless her in earth and heaven. Amen.

For My Father

Heavenly Father, as you sent your only Son into the world so long ago to accomplish your holy purposes, so my own father gave life, guidance, and protection within my family and then sent me forth. I give you thanks for that man to whom you entrusted fatherhood for my benefit and who has lived under your fatherly care all his days. As parent-hood may (or has) become my role in life, so let me live under the same blessing you afforded to my father. And through whatever struggles may come my way as I try to become a great parent from far away on this deployment, let me bless children as he blessed me in his day, and hear my prayer of thanks for him and his love for me. May he enjoy your grace abundantly, and in the life to come may he rejoice in your presence. Amen.

The Prayer of Kagawa

O Lord, revive thy Church, beginning with me. Amen.

Prayers for Others

PRAYING FOR OUR COUNTRY

We are embarked on our nation's business, and we serve under a chain of command led by the Commander-in-Chief of the Armed Forces, the President of the United States. Unless we are very junior in our service, we also stand between the President and those junior to us in the chain-of-command system.

Many people do not understand the words "power" and "authority," and so they confuse the two. A great many citizens do not know where and how they fit into the system of relationships of their workplace or even their families—resulting in a conflict of roles and confusion of purpose in their lives.

Serving in the Armed Forces really does clarify living for us. Before the prayers for our country, here are two short scriptures about understanding one's place *and learning how to be a student of one's place and role—one about Jesus himself and one about a centurion in the Roman Army. We know who Jesus is, but look at how he understands his role. The centurion is a career soldier, perhaps best understood as a Warrant Officer, but look at how he understands his role compared to that of Jesus.*

The first item comes from Philippians 2:5-8—a segment commonly called the Carmen Christi*—the Song of Christ. Within the* Carmen Christi*, it is said of Jesus and applied to the rest of us:*

Let the same mind be in you that was in Christ Jesus, who, though he was in the form of God, did not regard equality with God as something to be exploited, but emptied himself, taking the form of a slave, being born in human likeness. And being found in human form, he humbled himself and became obedient to the point of death—even death on a cross.

The second item comes from Luke 7:6-9, in which the centurion is in need of Jesus' help to heal his domestic servant but considers himself unworthy of the attention of someone as senior as the Messiah. He had probably learned that lesson by bad experience with senior officers along the way! The whole episode is worth reading, but here is the segment about the chain-of-command:

And Jesus went with them, but when he was not far from the house, the centurion sent friends to say to him, "Lord, do not trouble yourself, for I am not worthy to have you come under my roof; therefore I did not presume to come to you. But only speak the word, and let my servant be healed. For I also am a man set under authority, with soldiers under me; and I say to one, 'Go,' and he goes, and to another, 'Come,' and he comes, and to my slave, 'Do this,' and the slave does it." When Jesus heard this he was amazed at him, and turning to the crowd that followed him, he said, "I tell you, not even in Israel have I found such faith."

Civilians would never want you to know this, but take it to heart: the level of faith that lets us serve daily in the armed forces far exceeds anything that the civilians understand.

For the United States of America

Almighty God, who hast given us this good land for our heritage: We humbly beseech thee that we may always prove ourselves a people mindful of thy favor and glad to do thy will. Bless our land with honorable industry, sound learning, and pure manners. Save us from violence, discord, and confusion; from pride and arrogance, and from every evil way. Defend our liberties, and fashion into one united people the multitudes brought hither out of many kindreds and tongues. Endue with the spirit of wisdom those to whom in thy Name we entrust the authority of government, that there may be justice and peace at home, and that, through obedience to thy law, we may show forth thy praise among the nations of the earth. In the time of prosperity, fill our hearts with thankfulness, and in the day of trouble, suffer not our trust in thee to fail; all which we ask through Jesus Christ our Lord. Amen.

For the President of the United States
and all in Civil Authority

O Lord our Governor, whose glory is in all the world: We commend this nation to thy merciful care, that, being guided by thy Providence, we may dwell secure in thy peace. Grant to the President of the United States, the Governor of this State (or Commonwealth), and to all in authority, wisdom and strength to know and to do thy will. Fill them with the love of truth and righteousness, and make them ever mindful of their calling to serve this people in thy fear; through Jesus Christ our Lord, who liveth and reigneth with thee and the Holy Spirit, one God, world without end. Amen.

For those who serve in the Armed Forces

Almighty God, we commend to your gracious care
    and keeping
all the men and women of our armed forces at
    home and abroad.
Defend them day by day with your heavenly grace;
strengthen them in their trials and temptations;

give them courage to face the perils which beset
    them;
and grant them a sense of your abiding presence
    wherever they may be;
through Jesus Christ our Lord. Amen.

"I Vow to Thee My Country"

I vow to thee, my country, all earthly things above,
Entire and whole and perfect, the service of my
    love:
The love that asks no question, the love that
    stands the test,
That lays upon the altar the dearest and the best;
The love that never falters, the love that pays the
    price,
The love that makes undaunted the final sacrifice.

And there's another country, I've heard of long ago,
Most dear to them that love her, most great to
    them that know;
We may not count her armies, we may not see her
    King;

Her fortress is a faithful heart, her pride is
    suffering;
And soul by soul and silently her shining bounds
    increase,
And her ways are ways of gentleness and all her
    paths are peace.

"All Through The Night"
Ar Hyd y Nos

> "All through the Night" does not translate easily into
> English from Welsh. There are many variants, but
> here is a modern translation by J. Mark Sugars and
> singable to the traditional tune.

Sleep my love, and peace attend thee
All through the night.
Guardian angels God will lend thee,
All through the night.

Soft the drowsy hours are creeping,
Hill and vale in slumber steeping,
I my loving vigil keeping,
All through the night.

Angels watching ever round thee,
All through the night,
In thy slumbers close surround thee,
All through the night.

They should of all fears disarm thee,
No forebodings should alarm thee,
They will let no peril harm thee,
All through the night.

O God, our heavenly Father, as the evening
shadows fall and the darkness gathers around us,
grant us a peaceful night and a quiet resting place.
Deliver us, O Lord, from the excitement and cares of
the toilsome day, the pressures of worldly anxieties,
and the restlessness of the world. Grant to the
young, serious thought; to the old, gratitude for
your mercies; to all who love you, a greater and
deeper love; to those who love you not, the beginning
of a better life which you alone can give. Father, be
with our families and loved ones from whom we
are separated. Assure them of our love and concern
and of your divine and holy presence. Amen.

Almighty Father, we've come to the end of another day. Lord, lights are important to a sailor at sea. Always before we became so electronically sophisticated and sometimes even in our day and age, a sailor navigated by the sun during the day and by the stars at night. Ships use running lights to avoid collisions at sea, and lighthouses and beacons warn us of dangerous rocks and shoals, while the lights of harbor signify safety and friends. Tonight, Lord, we pray that you may always be the guiding light of our transit through this earthly life. Bless our families and loved ones, grant us a peaceful rest, and Lord, let there be peace in our world. Amen.

Our Father, God and Creator, we turn again to you for refuge from the hustle and hurry of the world without, and from the fury and fears within. Help us, O God, to find that peace and rest which can be found only in you; that we may meet the future with grateful hearts, the difficulties with willingness. And keep us, Father, from petty irritations. We pray for those among us who have been struck by illness or misfortune, or who are suffering any trial; for those who have been taken from our midst; and especially for those loved ones and family who anxiously await our return. May you keep both them and us in the palm of your protecting hand, this night and evermore. Amen.

For My Command's Chaplains

Grant, Almighty God, your help and strength to those whom you have called and sent to minister to your people in (my service) and here in (my command). Give my fine and honorable enough grace and power to make full proof of their ministry and to fulfill the duties you have entrusted to them. Help them to give themselves entirely to you and your mission, that glorifying you in holiness of life, they may lead many of us to your life and service; through Jesus Christ our Lord. Amen.

Praying and Singing for
My Branch of Service

Loyalty to our own branch of the service is a sign that we belong to the team and that we stand by all those others who serve alongside us. "There are no former Marines," said a Marine Colonel who was a fellow deployer. "Once a Marine, always a Marine," said another.

The Sergeant Major, said, "Nobody never recovers from being first addressed as 'Marine.'"

The 13th Commandant of the Marine Corps, General John Archer Lejeune, described the experience of joining the Corps as such a life-defining change that one remains stronger and better as long as life endures and there is a job to be done—some continuing to serve in the Corps and many return to civilian life to build a stronger America.

Enough about Marines. The point is that all of our armed forces strengthen our personalities and raise our patriotic loyalties to a level that can be achieved in no other way. None of us should ever recover from those powerful experiences of life in a uniform that builds us, and that is a good thing for ourselves, our families, and our country. May it always be so!

Prayers for our services abound, and here is a small and incomplete collection of them. Creativity has not exhausted all the good ideas, so feel free to write more of your own and share them.

In Time of War and Tumult

Almighty God, the supreme Governor of all things, whose power no creature is able to resist, to whom it belongeth justly to punish sinners, and to be merciful to those who truly repent: Save and deliver us, we humbly beseech thee, from the hands of our enemies; that we, being armed with thy defense, may be preserved evermore from all perils, to glorify thee, who art the only giver of all victory; through the merits of thy Son, Jesus Christ our Lord. Amen.

For the Army
(The Army birthday is 14 June 1775)

O Lord God of Hosts, stretch forth, we pray thee, thine almighty arm to strengthen and protect the soldiers of our country; Support them in the day of battle, and in the time of peace keep them safe from all evil; endue them with courage and loyalty; and grant that in all things they may serve without reproach; through Jesus Christ our Lord. Amen.

<hr />

For the Navy
(The Navy birthday is 13 October 1775)

O Eternal Lord God, who alone spreadest out the heavens, and rulest the raging of the sea; vouchsafe to take into thy almighty and most gracious protection our country's Navy, and all who serve therein. Preserve them from the dangers of the sea, and from the violence of the enemy; that they may be a safeguard unto the United States of America, and a security for such as pass on the seas upon their lawful occasions; that the inhabitants of our land may in peace and quietness serve thee our God, to the glory of thy Name; through Jesus Christ our Lord. Amen.

<hr />

The Marine's Prayer
(The Marine Corps birthday is 10 November 1775)

Almighty Father, whose command is over all and whose love never fails, make me aware of thy presence and obedient to thy will. Keep me true to my best self, guarding me against dishonesty in purpose and deed and helping me to live so that I can face my fellow Marines, my loved ones and thee without shame or fear. Protect my family. Give me the will to do the work of a Marine and to accept my share of responsibilities with vigor and enthusiasm. Grant me the courage to be proficient in my daily performance. Keep me loyal and faithful to my superiors and to the duties my country and the Marine Corps have entrusted to me. Make me considerate of those committed to my leadership. Help me to wear my uniform with dignity, and let it remind me daily of the traditions which I must uphold. If I am inclined to doubt, steady my faith; if I am tempted, make me strong to resist; if I should miss the mark, give me courage to try again. Guild me with the light of truth and grant me wisdom by which I may understand this answer to my prayer. Amen.

For the Air Force
(The Air Force birthday is 18 September 1947)

O Lord of hosts, you stretch out the heavens like a curtain: Watch over and protect, we pray, the aviators of the United States Air Force as they fly on their appointed missions and all on the ground who make their flights safe and possible. Give them courage as they face the foe, and skill to bring their aircraft back safely. Endow all who make aviation possible with skill and careful attention to their role in the larger community of the Air Force. Sustain Air Force families with your everlasting arms. May your strong arm strengthen them, your right hand hold them up, and your wisdom guide them home, that they may return to the earth and their homeland with a grateful sense of your mercy; and all through the goodness of our Lord Jesus. Amen.

A Coast Guard Prayer
(The Coast Guard birthday is 4 August 1790)

Almighty and Everlasting God, whose hand stills the tumult of the deep, we offer our prayers for those who serve in our Coast Guard. We are mindful of their traditions of selfless service to the seafarers who make their ways to appointed ports. Employ their devotions of good ends as they track the weather and search the seas for those in extremity of storm, shipwreck or battle. Make their soundings and markings sure that safe passages may be found by those who go down to the sea in ships. Encourage them, O Lord, as they stand guard over our coasts and the bulwarks of our freedoms. Graciously deliver them from threatening calamities in all their perilous voyages. Bless the keepers of the lights and be thou their close friend in lonely watches. Keep the beacons of honor and duty burning that they may reach the home port with duty well performed, in service to thee and our land. Amen.

PRAYING FOR THOSE WHOM WE LEAD

*People who we serve through our own leadership hold
us in high esteem, even if they do not say so directly.
We may think like this in our quiet moments: "My
people think I know everything. It isn't true! I learn
something new every day, and some of the most important learnings come from those good people who look
to me for leadership. May my workshop, classroom, or
office be a place where my people get what they really
need. May I be gifted to provide it for them, and may
I be proud to see them grow, mature, and prosper.
And if the day of battle should come—when we do
what we trained to do and hope to never actually
do—may I not have failed those good people. I really
do love them, but I cannot actually say so!"*

*Commanding Officers:
Praying for their People*

Lord, wisdom is such an elusive thing!

It is more than information: it is akin to knowledge, it is broader than truth, more satisfying than
experience. It is captured to some extent by insight,
and emerges occasionally through well thought-out
opinion. To become a wise person is to know all of
these—and more. It is the ability to know myself as
a leader and as merely myself:

My mind open,
My heart free,
My feelings genuine,

All of my relationships in proper order—with my family, my loved ones at home; with my country; with these fine people I command; with others; and with you. Give me wisdom, O Lord. It is hard to find out here, but these fine people look for me to provide it. And so I look to you to be the source of it. Amen.

Departmental Leaders:
Praying for their People

Lord, we've heard that we are to be our brother's keeper. Some of us are burdened with deep concerns that worry the mind or hurt the heart. They may not always ask for help because it may be hard to talk about in the hearing of others, but they always need our understanding when things aren't going right. Lord, make me a listener when my people call out; a picker-upper when they fall; a sympathetic shoulder when they need a friend; and a keeper when they need strength. Amen.

Into your hands, Lord God, I commend my department to you this day. Let your presence be with all of us until its end. Enable us to feel that in doing our work we are doing your will, and that in serving others we are serving you; through Jesus Christ our Lord. Amen.

A Favorite Prayer of the
103rd Archbishop of Canterbury, George Carey

Lord Jesus Christ,
The Master Carpenter of Nazareth:
On a cross, through wood and nails, you have wrought man's salvation.
Wield well your tools in this workshop, so that we who come to you rough hewn, may by you be fashioned according to your will; for the sake of your tender mercy. Amen.

For Those Who Teach and Train Others

Why did you fill my classroom with such bright students, good Lord? They are the favorite sons and daughters of American families, and the truth is that they are smarter and stronger than I am. I have been there and done it, and they will be going there soon. Please make my classroom a place of honorable and honest learning, an industrious place of challenge and achievement, a hospitable place where every question is welcome, and a godly place of good learning and good manners. And when we have finished this course together, send these great young people to work, where they may be better than I was. Amen.

Lord, we stand in awe at the thought of how greatly you respect us.

You offer us life and love, but you do not force yourself upon us.

Life is opened wide for us,

We are free to love, and free not to love.

Free to give, and free to seek only for ourselves.

Breathe your spirit on all who are serving here with me tonight that in all the choices we face, we may never run from life or from love in fear, but freely be able to risk for your sake. Amen.

⚜

Good Lord—deliver us.

The promotions list comes out soon, and the days of waiting are almost over; some will receive greater rank, pay, and responsibility; some will not. We pray for all of them—that those selected will accept our praise as acknowledgment of their achievement and readiness for new responsibilities; and for those who are passed over, that they will continue to be aware of their value to us and to you, and in not losing heart, to continue to strive for their chosen goals. Protect us through the night, and our loved ones, wherever they may be in your vast kingdom. And grant us peace in our time. Amen.

⚜

Dear God in Heaven, grant to us a warm heart that we may bless hurt lives. Challenge our complacency so that we may accomplish what seems out of reach. May we be inspired enough today, that what we do makes a difference tomorrow. And may we not overlook your many gifts to us, the moments of each day; the rising of each opportunity; and the human needs which capture our attention. Amen.

Eternal God, we are beginning exercises which require a commitment to cooperation. Help us to realize that we cannot operate alone. Leaders need men and women, and we need leaders. Make us sense our basic unity of purpose and help us to see that each person's welfare is intimately tied to the welfare of the whole command, and that all of us depend upon the well-being of each other. Fill us with love that knows no barrier, with understanding that reaches all, with courage that cannot be shaken, with strength sufficient to our tasks, with wisdom to meet life's complexities, with power to lift us to you. Amen.

Today we remember, dear Lord God, those whose work is not in the limelight or spotlight— those who sometimes get the idea that because they are not singled out, they are not appreciated. While they may go unheralded or unapplauded, help them realize that they are appreciated, and that if they did not do their work, this mission would stop. Help them to know there are no insignificant jobs but only some people who do jobs insignificantly. May each of us hear your words: Just as I was with Moses, I will be with you; I will not fail you or forsake you. Amen.

Lord, it's been a busy and productive day. A lot of people put a lot of effort into their jobs. We're grateful for their hard work. And now, as darkness closes in, grant them a peaceful night and a quiet rest. Deliver them from the cares of a busy day, the pressures of the job, and worry about those they love at home. Through this night, and again on the morrow, may a sense of your presence continue to sustain them as they try to do their best. Amen.

Praying for Our Own Command

"Where are you stationed?" one is asked. The answer is always the name of the organization where we are assigned and the location. Whether we like the command or detest it, it is our home and the place where we belong.

Some say that the best command of all was our first one, and we measure all others by comparison. The next best is the one we hope will come with our next transfer order. The worst one is clearly the current one. Of course, such wisdom is untrue.

Especially for those in leadership, it is a privilege to offer our current command to God for his blessing. It is a profound gift to pray for those who are senior to us for leadership, wisdom, and strength.

O Lord our God, our thoughts are about families and loved ones as our family readiness group meets tonight. We're about as far away from them as we can be. We think of the times we took them for granted when we could see them every day. But now that we're apart, we realized more than ever how much meaning they give to our lives. Especially tonight we pray for those who have received by mail or message news of family illness or death. Our prayer always is that as those on duty stand watch right now, you will continue to watch over us and those we love. Amen.

⁂

As day turns to night, we pause to pray for those whose joy has turned to sorrow, especially for our comrades who received news of illness, injury or death in their family circle. We remind them of the words of the prophet Isaiah: "They that wait upon the Lord shall renew their strength, they shall mount up with wings like eagles, they shall run and not be wary, they shall walk and not faint." Into your care, and with this prayer, we commend our friends to you for renewal of their strength. As those on duty stand watch, continue to watch over us and those we love. Amen.

⁂

Lord, a lot of living goes on during the course of a week for the crew and the loved ones of a command of this size: some dying, and a little hurting, too . . . and we have had our share this week. So, tonight we bring our needs before you: for those whose names we mention now. . .and some only you can know about.

If we are blind . . . we ask for sight.

If we are afraid . . . we ask for courage.

If we are discouraged . . . we ask for hope.

If we are threatened . . . we ask for faith and for strength.

Lesser people might fold . . . but not us, Lord . . . not as long as you are with us; Lord, be with us all. Amen.

God, the workload and the workdays out here are staggering. There are long days of work and short times of rest. Help us to offer the work we do as a prayer to you. There are many ways one can pray. There is the prayer of the greasy mechanic and the prayer of the white-robed monk. One prays with his hands and back; the other on his knees. Accept our work today as our prayers. Amen.

God, we're busy with many things around here. The jobs overlap; the days overlap; sometimes we feel lost in a maze, unnoticed by anyone else. Then there are times we get caught up in our own little worlds—our shop, our piece of equipment, aircraft, or vehicle, or division—and fail to notice or even care about each other. This great command can be very impersonal. Help us to realize that we are important in your eyes and that we are important to one another. Amen.

God, tonight we do not ask so much for a reduction of our work, as we ask for strength to do the work given us. We do not ask so much for deliverance from life's misfortunes, as we ask for faith to see us through difficult times. We do not ask so much for relief from our loneliness and boredom, as we ask for the ability to cheer the discouraged and to provide friendship to each other. Let this be the prayer from our hearts tonight, for we know that as those on duty stand watch, you will watch over us and those we love. Amen.

Lord, at the end of your long, busy week you took a day off and rested. It doesn't look like we can do that, but we can make the most of a few quiet moments here and there. Help us to use quiet times profitably, prayerfully, as those who are thoughtful about their lives, their goals, and their ambitions. Raise our sights; help us find a purpose in our work. And Lord, if in our rushing about this place so far from home and family we forget you, please—do not forget us. Amen.

Transitional Times

GOING HOME SOON

Your author remembers flying back to the States with a deploying unit for the first time. One might assume that everybody was happy about going home and that the whole scene was a party atmosphere. Not so!

Most folks were delighted to be going home to welcoming families and time off to enjoy them. A small number were going home to disastrous personal situations. Some had no idea about whether there would be anybody waiting to greet them—or not.

Pay attention to the others around you, especially those trying to hide their worry and prevent their anxiety from disrupting the joy of others. Pray for them—they need it, and you can afford it.

If you are going home to delightful greetings and good times with family, do enjoy the reunion. Fall in love with your spouse all over again. You earned it, and you deserve it. Be sure to read and talk about the end of the first chapter of this book before you arrive.

Almighty God, on the eve of our return home, help us to understand that our longest journey is the journey inward. May we, therefore, return home knowing that we did nobly what we must, in spite of personal consequences, in spite of obstacles and pressures. Let us never forget that the energy, the faith and devotion that we brought to this endeavor, will light our country and that the glow from that fire can truly keep the light of freedom alive. Amen.

Teach us, O Lord, to appreciate the little things which have touched our lives while deployed so far from home in these last months—routine duty, a card game, small talk with our shipmates. May we live deeply, drinking of the fountains that are all about us. We thank you for the beauty of this night and the fellowship that we enjoy. Watch over our loved ones as we quiet ourselves for this last night away. Bless us with such a homecoming tomorrow that the loneliness of separation will be quickly changed into the joy of reunion. Amen.

Thank you, Lord, for staying with us, for making your course our course, our course yours. You have brought us through tropical heat, water spouts, gamma globulin shots, malaria pills, water restriction hours, no showers, lost and stuck tour buses, urban thieves, terrorist slander, sea sickness and, Lord, if you can just get us through this last cold weather to the safety of homeport, to our families and friends, you might say we owe you one. Yes, we do! Amen.

Lord, we've had another full day of demanding work. We're grateful it passed without serious injury. We feel a bit like a runner nearing the end of a marathon. We're tired, but we can see the finish line. Many will be working hard through the night to complete jobs or packing. Some will be watching TV. Not many will sleep. Although the deployment isn't over 'til it's over, we're pulling into home with anticipation and enthusiasm. Good night, Lord. Amen.

Lord, we give thanks tonight for all those who have loved us and have shown us an example of faithful and godly living. We are grateful for those who have shown kindness when things were tough, those who helped when we couldn't help ourselves, and those who loved us when we didn't feel lovable. As our thoughts turn more and more toward home and our families there, we pray especially for those who have special anxieties about returning home. Help each of us to use the days ahead to prepare ourselves for homecoming. Amen.

Lord, you had a purpose for each of us as we
    began this deployment.
Did you want us to test our skills and face difficult
    challenges?
Did you want us to learn to work with others who
    have different ideas—different ways?

Did you want us to realize how much those back
    home mean to us?
Did you want to stretch our patience?
Did you want us to accept what we could not
    change?
Well, Lord, that's what happened.
Your purpose has been made clear to us, and our
    prayers have been answered.
Thank you, Lord, good night and Amen.

As the days pass by quickly, and the nights fly on by,
We'll soon be hitting homeport. The time is
    drawing nigh.
We'll have friends and loved ones, waiting on the
    shore.
And as we step upon the pier, they'll wait for us
    no more.
Lord, comfort our anxiety, and give us patience, too.
For though we seek our loved ones, we still have
    need of you.
Lord, we all are getting "channel fever,"
We ask you to bless us with a deep, unbroken sleep.
Thank you, Lord. Amen.

Eternal God, as we move out of the strain of the doing into the joy of the having done, we have come to realize that what we do on some great occasion has probably depended on what we already were; and what we now become depends on how we order our lives. Each act of our lives casts a shadow forward into the next day. Dear God, you've blessed our efforts of this cruise and thus we end this prayer, this day and this deployment with anticipation for tomorrow and a sincere gratitude for our yesterdays. Amen.

LEAVING THE COMMAND OR THE SERVICE ALTOGETHER

It is all finished, or it will soon be. Remember what is often attributed to that great American philosopher Yogi Berra: "The game ain't over 'till it's over!" Eventually it is over—either that expeditionary deployment outside of the States or even your period of service. Whatever the occasion, it is a time of mixed joy and stress—always true at times of change. Your God, who has been faithful to you all along, will go with you and be faithful in your future, too.

Dear God: Help me be a good sport in this game of life. I don't ask for any easy place in the lineup. Put me anywhere you need me. I only ask that I can give you a hundred percent of everything I have. If all the hard drives seem to come my way, I thank you for the compliment. Help me remember that you never send a player more trouble than can be handled. So it has been and always will be—world without end. Amen.

May we in this command be able to say that we matched our country's military restraint with our own moral restraint, our nation's wealth with our wisdom, its power with our purpose; so that, in the end, we can echo the words now millennia old and spoken by St. Paul at the end of his own career: "I have fought a good fight, I have run the full distance, and I have kept the faith." Amen.

Dear God, we can count the seeds in an apple, but you alone can count the apples in a seed! Help us to realize the possibilities of one fertile idea; enable us to set great goals for ourselves, not to cover us as an overhead but to lift us up to greater attempts. And, even if we fall short, teach us that failure doesn't mean we have wasted ourselves, but that we have an excuse to start again. With your grace help us dare to try. Amen.

Prayers of the Heroes

There are heroes who bear arms, and there are heroes who win their battles as they model Jesus Christ in their lives. Here is a collection of prayers that are attached to the names of heroes communicating their faith to us across the ages. Not all the attributions are necessarily true or can be verified, but these people communicate to us across the ages by the prayers they left behind.

We only see vaguely into the Kingdom of God. One way we try is to understand how we stand on the shoulders of the saints and heroes and try to peer over a fence to see what is happening on the other side. Let's listen. If you have others to add, please send a note to your author.

THE PRAYER ATTRIBUTED TO
ST. FRANCIS OF ASSISI

Lord, make us instruments of your peace.
Where there is hatred, let us sow love;
where there is injury, pardon;
where there is discord, union;
where there is doubt, faith;
where there is despair, hope;
where there is darkness, light;
where there is sadness, joy.
Grant that we may not so much seek to be
    consoled as to console;
to be understood as to understand;
to be loved as to love.
For it is in giving that we receive;
it is in pardoning that we are pardoned;
and it is in dying that we are reborn to eternal life.
    Amen.

The Prayer of
St. Richard of Chichester

Thanks be to thee, O Lord Jesus Christ,
for all the cruel pains and insults thou hast borne
    for us;
for all the many blessings thou hast won for us.
O holy Jesus, most merciful Redeemer, friend and
    brother,
may we know thee more clearly,
love thee more dearly,
and follow thee more nearly, day by day. Amen.

The Prayer of St. Ignatius Loyola

Teach us, good Lord, to serve thee as thou deservest;
to give and not to count the cost;
to fight and not to heed the wounds;
to toil and not to seek for rest;
to labor and to ask for no reward
save that of knowing that we do thy will. Amen.

Sir Francis Drake's Prayer

O Lord, when thou givest to thy servants to endeavor in any great matter, grant us also to know that it is not the beginning but the continuing of the same until to be thoroughly finished that yieldeth the true glory; through him who for the finishing of thy work laid down his life, Jesus Christ our Lord. Amen.

King Alfred's Prayer

Lord God Almighty, we pray thee for thy great mercy to guide us to thy will, to make our minds steadfast, to strengthen us against temptation, to put all evil far from us. Shield us against our foes, seen and unseen; teach us that we may inwardly love thee before all things with a clean mind and a clean body; for thou art our Maker and Redeemer, our help and our strength, our trust and our hope, now and for ever. Amen.

LIEUTENANT GENERAL GEORGE S. PATTON'S THIRD ARMY PRAYER 8 DECEMBER 1944

Penned by Army Chaplain James H. O'Neill, Senior Chaplain of the Third Army.

Chaplain O'Neill quoted General Patton as having instructed him: "Urge all of your men to pray, not alone in church, but everywhere. Pray when driving. Pray when fighting. Pray alone. Pray with others. Pray by night and pray by day. Pray for the cessation of immoderate rains, for good weather for battle. Pray for the defeat of our wicked enemy whose banner is injustice and whose good is oppression. Pray for victory. Pray for our Army, and pray for peace."

Almighty and most merciful Father, we humbly beseech thee, of thy great goodness, to restrain these immoderate rains with which we have had to contend. Grant us fair weather for battle. Graciously hearken to us as soldiers who call thee that, armed with thy power, we may advance from victory to victory, and crush the oppression and wickedness of our enemies, and establish thy justice among men and nations. Amen.

A Prayer of St. Chrysostom

Almighty God, you have given us grace at this time with one accord to make our common supplication to you; and you have promised through your well-beloved Son that when two or three are gathered together in his Name you will be in the midst of them: Fulfill now, O Lord, our desires and petitions as may be best for us; granting us in this world knowledge of your truth, and in the age to come life everlasting. Amen.

Resources within
the Bible

You do have a Bible available, don't you? No? The
Chaplain in your unit has brought plenty of them and
will gladly give you a copy for the asking. There are
probably some in a literature rack at the Chaplain's
Office. Go get one of your own. One great outcome
of the Protestant Reformation and development of
the printing press is that we all can have a copy of
our own and read it in our own language.

Okay, you have one now. It's a pretty big book—
a library, really. What will you read? Here is a
shopping list of helpful scriptures. Only a few really
important passages and a few psalms are quoted in
this book, because you can look up others easily. The
Bible is a very rich book, so this or any reading list is
incomplete. People around you will be happy to steer
you to passages they find most helpful. This list is in
order of the Bible text.

Exodus 20:1–17 The Ten Commandments.

Deuteronomy 6:4–9 The Shema Ysreal, the single most important learning in Jewish scriptures—the important practice of bringing your faith into the center of your life and keeping it there—quoted by Jesus as the Great Commandment.

Psalms Helpful selections are scattered throughout this book.

Proverbs Practical and handy wisdom; a great many topics.

Isaiah 40:1–8 Early announcement of activity leading to John the Baptist and the birth of Jesus; words of comfort to God's exiled people.

Isaiah 40:31 Important memory verse in times of trouble.

Isaiah 42:1–6 God's servant, an early prophecy of the Messiah.

Isaiah 55:6–11 Seeking God, for his word is power and effective to accomplish things.

Isaiah 61:1–3 Read by Jesus in the Nazareth Synagogue, see Luke 4:18–19; prophecy of the Messiah fulfilled in Jesus.

Jeremiah 29:11–13 God has plans to prosper his people.

Matthew 5—7 The famous Sermon on the Mount, Jesus' teaching on a great many topics of practical application and holy living, especially important as the background of Christian ethics. Read and consider memorizing 5:1–12, The Beatitudes.

Matthew 28:16–20 Jesus' Great Commission to his disciples.

Luke 2:1–20 Birth of Jesus at Bethlehem; the Christmas story.

John 3:16–17 Well-known and profoundly important statement of God's purpose in sending his son Jesus into the world.

John 14:1–6 Words of comfort in troubled times, especially when someone close to you has died.

John 18—19 Jesus' death at the Cross. Also in Matthew 27, Mark 15, Luke 23.

John 20:1–9 Easter, Jesus raised from death. Also in Matthew 28, Mark 16, Luke 24.

Acts 2:1–21 Pentecost, the Holy Spirit comes to the apostles.

Acts 10 Conversion of the first Gentile Christian—Cornelius the centurion, a Roman career soldier.

Romans 8:31–39 The power of God withstanding the evil powers of the world.

Romans 10:17 Where faith comes from and how it is built.

Romans 12:9–13 Practicing your religion with zeal.

1 Corinthians 12:8–13 Spiritual gifts, their one source and many forms.

1 Corinthians 13 St. Paul writes his experience of the importance of love and virtues in the community.

Ephesians 6:10–18 Putting on the whole armor of God and maintaining readiness in faith, quoted in the chapter on personal readiness of this book.

Philippians 4:5–13 St. Paul teaches from experience about focus and endurance under trial of imprisonment and of learning to prosper spiritually in the worst of circumstances.

1 Timothy 1:15 St. Paul teaches why Jesus Christ came into the world.

1 Timothy 1:18–19 and *6:11–12* St. Paul equipping Timothy for leadership and endurance; turning his mission over to Timothy.

2 Timothy 4:1–8 St. Paul passing authority and wisdom to Timothy; change of command completed.

Hebrews 13:8 The Lord Jesus Christ is constant, sure, dependable.

Hebrews 13:17 Good reason to support your chain of command.

Hebrews 13:20–21 A blessing for you and to you.

James 1:19–20 and 3:4 The wisdom of not speaking in anger and measuring your response to provocation.

James 3:13–18 and 4:7–8 The problem of evil and the importance of focusing to resist it.

1 Peter 2:9–10 You are a chosen people; live accordingly.

1 Peter 5:8–9 Be self-controlled and alert; beware of spiritual danger—and be ready.

1 John 3:1–12 Why we should love one another.

1 John 4:1–6 Test spiritual ideas; a short test to check for the Spirit of God.

Revelation 22:18–21 End of the Bible; importance of the whole integrity of the Bible for holy living.

www.ingramcontent.com/pod-product-compliance
Lightning Source LLC
Jackson TN
JSHW011937131224
75386JS00041B/1430

* 9 7 8 0 8 9 8 6 9 5 8 7 8 *